Unfinished Stories!

A Tale of Hazara Genocide in Pakistan

Author:
Hassan Raza Changezi

Lead Translators:
Sajjad Hussain Changezi
Zahra Shah

Dedication

To all those people who raised voice against the
Hazara Genocide regardless of race, colour,
creed, religion and regional boundaries and
displayed unwavering solidarity with the Hazara
community during some of the most difficult
times.

Funding: The translation and publication of this book is funded by Aikafund : www.aikafund.org

Name of Publication: Unfinished Stories! (Translation)
Author: Hassan Raza Changezi

Lead Translators:
Sajjad Hussain Changezi
Zahra Shah

ISBN: 978-969-7683-01-7

Front Cover image by: Syed Muhammad Hussain
Book designed by: Saeed Ibrahim
Photo Courtesy: Asef Ali Mohammad

Publisher: Nirvan Publication House
Printer: Shirkat Printing Press, Lahore

Date of Publication: August, 2022
Price in Pakistan: Rs. 800/-
International : $20

Acknowledgment

We are deeply grateful to our team of volunteers who selflessly dedicated a lot of time to translate, review the work of their peers, and proofread the translated drafts. First, we would like to thank Syed Inayat for his contribution to this project in multiple roles. He has remained a source of motivation throughout, and we cannot thank him enough. We are grateful to Fatima Hashmi for connecting us to Asad Khan Betani. Betani Sb from Zhob extended solidarity across the ethnic and sectarian lines and contributed to this project. We are thankful to the super talented Mohammad Atif who has translated and reviewed some of the most difficult essays in this book. A very special thanks to Farman Kakar for proofreading the book. Needless to mention that he has always played an active role in raising voice against our genocide. Finally, we are immensely grateful to Akram Gizabi and Abbas Changezi for their contribution throughout. We would like to thank 'Aikafund' for funding the publication of this book. Aikafund is a Danish NGO operating in Afghanistan and Pakistan. The fund helps school children and university students with physical aids like educational materials, fees and other expenses needed for proper schooling. Last and most importantly, thanks to Hassan Sb for writing these stories as a spokesperson of his generation of the Hazaras in Quetta. Our team has only attempted to take his narration of painful Quetta incidents to wider audience across time and space. Maybe 50 years from now, a grand daughter of ours, a Pakistan history scholar or a human rights researcher will sip a cup of coffee in a safe and cozy space in a library somewhere in Sydney or Karachi, and realize it was not easy to be a Hazara and live through 2012 to 2015 in Quetta, Pakistan.

Sajjad Hussain Changezi
Zahra Shah

Contents

Book Review:

Note from the Translators

Sajjad Hussain Changezi

"Unfinished Stories" has remained my major fight for a greater part of the year 2020. For multiple reasons, translation of this book posed significant challenges. If you agree with me that fan-boyhood can affect the professional work and collegiality, this is the first. Hassan Raza Changezi is a public intellectual and an author of many books in Urdu and Dari. He stepped in the world of non-fiction literature as a translator himself and his translation of L. Temirkhanov's "History of Hazara Mughals" remains one of the books that has shaped me, my sense of identity and political conscience. On top of that, his mastery over the language of Urdu and his poetic style for serious essays make it an especially challenging task to offer a stylistic translation without departing from the original message. Since his translation of Temikhanov's, I have not ceased to follow Hassan Raza Changezi for insight and inspiration. I have remained an avid reader of his articles, blogs and essays as he stepped up during the most depressing of the years. With his writings, Hassan Sb has taught our generation how the unheard perspectives of the oppressed nations can be articulated to register protest. In the face of the genocidal violence that Hazara population in Quetta, Pakistan have faced during the last two decades and which peaked around 2009-14, these articles of Hassan Sb's are documents of historical importance. The essays in this collection are for our next generations who we all hope are privileged enough to breathe and grow up in safer times and societies so that when they are bothered to dig, they can learn about the battles their forefathers and foremothers fought. If these stories traveled that far, it would mean we have not given up. If we have not given up, we cannot have lost.

The realization that the younger generation of Hazaras across the globe will be the ultimate judges for these notes, has put additional burden on our shoulders to produce a document of international standing. Within the environment that this team of translators has operated in, we have tried not to be discouraged by the absence of a robust culture of standard literary works. Through this literary project, this team of voluntary translators has set a precedent. How high are we able to set the bar? That is for you, the readers, to judge.

In translating this collection of published essays, journalistic articles and literary blog pieces, our goal was to produce a book in a universal language which should ideally be complete in itself without leaving its readers dearly missing genuine details from the original text. This vision can potentially put us at risk of being at odds with the fans of Hassan Sb who would have the academic zeal of juxtaposing both the Urdu and the English texts and point to anomalies. In our defense, Urdu is a language of high culture where a lot of meaning is conveyed through proverbs, poetic phrases, historic figures and symbols, literary jokes and indirect hints. I also believe this tradition has flourished in part because of the lack of freedom of expression which might have encouraged opinionmakers in the sub-continent to tempt their readers to capture their key message in between the lines.

A significant addition is that of the references and footnotes which the Urdu book has none. We do realize that this book is for wider audience who would need evidence in support of the arguments and claims made by the author. The essays in this collection were originally written between 2012 to 2015 and hence, we have preferred to include references from the media reports of those years. In some cases, where those reports are no longer available which is true for many Pakistani Urdu newspaper archives we have not shied away from using supporting evidence from media reports of later times. For referencing, we have followed the Chicago Manual of Style and we hope the footnotes will particularly help the researcher community. ■

Zahra Shah

It all began in the late 2000s. Those were some of the gloomiest days in our (Hazaras') history when our community members were the perpetual targets of terrorism in Quetta, Pakistan. Living thousands of miles away, we, the Hazara diaspora community, could do nothing but to mourn in silence; our eyes fixed to the tv screens; our hearts aching and praying for the peace of our hometown, Quetta.

To overcome the overwhelming feeling of grief or perhaps to register our protest, all we could do was to organize demonstrations and vigils. My daughter, alongside the other kids in our community, started coming to the protests with us even before she started going to school. She heard the terms 'terrorists', 'bomb-blasts' and 'genocide' first and learned their meanings later in life.

Growing up amidst all this chaos, she began asking questions, probably trying to figure out what was happening all around her, "Why do they want to kill us (the Hazaras)?" "What is our crime?" "What have we done to deserve this?" Following every incident, she would constantly ask such

11

questions. We, the otherwise very even-tempered and patient parents, started to feel increasingly exasperated as we had no answers to satisfy her inquisitive mind.

But now....... I suppose, we do. This book "Unfinished Stories" is the answer to most, if not all, of her questions and for that matter, of all those kids born to Hazara migrant parents outside Pakistan, who may or may not, one day, raise the same questions my daughter used to ask.

I am sure I speak for every team member when I say that we decided to translate this book mainly because we wanted these stories to travel to other parts of the world; touch people's minds and hearts; be heard; and be remembered. Having said that, the decision to translate Hassan Raza Changezi's book Qissa-hai-natamam was a haughty one, partly due to the lack of experience. But I'm glad we did it. And.......here we are! finally able to accomplish what we aspired. I can already feel that overwhelming sense of fulfilment!

Hassan Raza Changezi is one of the most prolific contemporary Hazara writers whom I admire for his simplistic yet captivating and subjective style of writing. Not only is he skilled in the art of grabbing readers' attention into the subject matter without using embellished language and sophisticated terminologies, but he also has proven his mastery over the Urdu language across different styles, from expository to narrative, from descriptive to persuasive; you name it.

"Unfinished Stories" is a collection of Hassan Raza Changezi's short stories, essays and blogs that portray the plight of our community and captures the stories of our ethnic cleansing. Through his writings, he shares his personal experiences; the very fact that gives these stories a sense of authenticity. As you read along, you feel a certain

12

sense of nostalgia in his tone when he recalls the days people from different belief systems lived in harmony, right before the society was pushed into the darkness of radicalisation. Moving on, you find yourself teary-eyed reading through the concerns of Uncle Abdul, the grief-stricken father of a bomb blast victim. As you proceed along, you come across the heart-wrenching wails of the mother of BUITEM's bomb blast victim. Through these stories, he skilfully captures the emotional trauma and excruciating pain a parent goes through in such tragic circumstances. In short, he does a wonderful job of elucidating the political, social, and economic ambience of our ethnic cleansing; from a perspective that does not appear as a cliche to the readers. Sobby stories or sentimental tales, whatever and however you label them, these stories make part of our painful history and define us as a community.

Being fully aware of the fact that the translated version is catering to the needs of a different audience, we have tried to use a language and style to resonate with the taste of target readers vis-a-vis making sure it has the same pulse as the original book. I found this whole translation journey a roller-coaster ride, literally. Oftentimes, we encountered challenges when dealing with linguistic expressions, idioms, sarcasm and poetry, among others. Some linguistic phrases are hard to explain in the target language as you cannot find an alternative version in the target language with the same concept. See this line, for instance.

اِدھر ڈوبے اُدھر نکلے ۔ اُدھر ڈوبے اِدھر نکلے

If you try to transcribe this phrase in its literal meaning, it may create ambiguity or misunderstanding or even the meaning can be lost altogether.

We faced a similar conundrum when dealing with satirical and sarcastic chapters due to different cultural and social sensitivities. It goes without saying that humour isn't the same everywhere. What is funny in one culture could be offensive in another culture.

Translation of poetry caused another set of dilemmas. Oftentimes, the words did not sync up because what rhymes in source language does not rhyme in the target language. Nothing can describe this situation as best as the words of the American poet Robert Frost, "Poetry is what gets lost in translation." However, we did our best to find matching words and making sure to transcribe the message as close to the original verses as we could. For example, see this one:

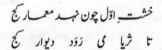

If you want to build your house properly,
Beware to lay the foundations correctly.
Or else you will get an unstable structure,
That may fall to the ground eventually.

Quite possibly, our work may not be completely error-free due to the variations in the syntax and grammar between the source and target languages; or even the differences in social and cultural contexts...... the list can be long. However, we have tried our best to transcribe the message as close and as accurate to the original manuscript as possible. ■

14

I

Sultan Rahi's Pakistan

ome 15 years ago, I had watched a ridiculous Pakistani film on my television screen (did I need to use the adjective "ridiculous"? Wouldn't "Pakistani film" suffice?). The film title was "Mister 420," a joke in itself. The movie was not memorable, yet there was one scene that refuses to go away from my memory. In that scene, the protagonist, the Lollywood equivalent of James Bond, Sultan Rahi[1], holds on to a pair of ropes to stop two running Japanese made HINO trucks with nothing but his bare hands. I laughed my lungs out watching that scene. The next day when I discussed the ridiculous scene with a friend, he did not show any sign of amusement. I was puzzled to see even such a nakedly unreal and ridiculously untrue depiction had failed to bring a faint reaction on his face. Upon inquiry, he responded by saying, "I have watched Sultan Rahi's film

[1]N Khan, "Sultan Rahi, Biography" IMDb,
https://www.imdb.com/name/nm0706691/bio

where he stopped the whole train with his bare hands."
I was shunned.

Above and beyond the laws of nature, Sultan Rahi was a hero who ruled imagination of Pakistani cinema goers for decades. In one moment, he would be shown touring around London and in the next, upon hearing his sister's cries for help, he would plunge right into the dark alley in a rural set up in Pakistani Punjab's Sheikhupura district. He would cover thousands of miles in a single leap and arrive just in time to neutralize his enemies. Dozens of AK-47 bullets would pierce his body, but nothing would keep him from finishing his action-loaded finale.

Alas, in real life, that very same heavenly hero could not survive a few bullets from his robbers. When faced with reality, nothing came to his rescue. No glimmer from his boastful film characters, none of his long echoing and earth-shattering dialogues, nothing helped him resist an unceremonious death at the hands a few robbers.[2]

Living a life divorced from reality and ultimately paying for this unforgivable mistake, it is not about one film actor, but the irony of Pakistan as a whole. In more ways than one, Sultan Rahi personifies Pakistani state and society. Right from the top executive and legislative bodies down to ordinary citizens, everybody is a mini Sultan Rahi in their own right. Just flip a few pages of our dailies and you will come across similar boastful

---

[2] M. Saeed Awan, "The mysterious murder of Sultan Rahi and other Lollywood tragedies", DAWN images, January 9, 2017, https://images.dawn.com/news/1176891

comments, "We have turned Pakistan into a nuclear power, we are the fortress of Islam, Pakistan's defence is undefeatable, our defence is in safe hands, we will blind the eyes that look at Pakistan with ill-intentions et cetera."

You are wrong if you believe our citizenry is more pacifist than our boastful politicians. Inflation, insecurity and lawlessness have turned our lives into hell and yet, we do not see a break in the chanting of boastful slogans; "We are a lively nation, we are here forever, how many of us can you kill? We are all ready to accept martyrdom et cetera."

It is worth having a glance at a country that boasts such claims. The same newspapers also report murders, targeted killings of minorities, high-profile assassinations, bombings and kidnappings for ransom. And then, his eminence, Rehman Malik, the interior minister puts all the blame on foreign actors, "Foreign hands are sabotaging peace in the country." What are you waiting for, why don't you blind the eyes looking at Pakistan with ill-intentions? This reminds me of Ardeshir Cowasjee, "We cannot fix our gutter... and yet, we campaign for the nuclear bomb."

Overall, we have failed miserably in our governance. However, we continue to issue warnings, threats, and boastful claims. We do not hesitate a second to blame foreign powers for whatever issues we fail to resolve. Forget about blinding the eyes of the enemies, in our moments of classic failures, we struggle to look them in the eye. Just recently, Mr. Malik issued another statement, "Some Islamic countries are fighting their proxy wars in our homeland." If you know this far, Honourable Minister, why don't you block them? It is an open secret that we do not have the guts to even protest their interference let alone blocking the patrons of these proxy wars. It's no less than a joke that an atomic power cannot even protest interference in its domestic affairs because it heavily depends on all the remittances and foreign aides (or charity, should I call?)

That is all that distinguishes the real world from the one we depict on our cinema screens. Someone conducts an operation right under our nose and safely escapes, and then we start accusing each other and covering up the issue rather than admitting loopholes in our defence and strategic systems. Law and order situation has worsened to a level where the government admitted, "A bunch of terrorists have hijacked the whole country and its 180 million people." And yet, there is no comprehensive, coordinated, and coherent plan to fight terrorism. Government, state institutions, politicians, all have conflicting narratives. Uncertainty, lawlessness, terrorism, and insecurity have victimised 180 million people. And yet, we continue to boast. While someone is taking the credit for the passing of 19th amendment, others are still in their motorway hangover. Some are fighting Dengue virus; others are celebrating the conclusion of Ashura processions without a mega incident of bombing (as if that bombing on Ashura processions is given!). On the one hand, there are people who hope the next elections will bring them their turn to loot the nation. On the other hand, there are others who promise to turn the country into Quaid-e Azam's Pakistan, i.e., back to 1947. I wonder if they really need to do that since our rulers and their strategic assets are already passionately advancing the project. If that is the picture at the centre, it is no better at the provincial and the local levels either. Our local leaders are the opportunists who have just got their turns after a lot of prayers and meditations. They are equally smart at making fake promises and issuing boastful statements.

In short, there is no shortage of fake promises and no end to boastings. I feel as if the movie "Mister 420" is being constantly televised everywhere. On the film screen, our heroes have managed to halt multiple trains with their bare hands. Sultan Rahi's boastings are echoing all around and a whole lot of 180 million people are frantically clapping and frantically screaming with amusement. This is truly Sultan Rahi's Pakistan.

December 12, 2012,

2

Pakistan, a Laboratory!

In this dear homeland of ours, just as we have a rich diversity in terms of fruits and vegetation, there is no dearth of political leaders and parties with conflicting narratives and sloganeers. What is common in them, however, is that all of them want to enjoy the perks and privileges of the executive. Some of them have already tasted power in some form while the rest have fixated their eyes on the upcoming political opportunities so that they can navigate through chaos and find themselves on the treasury benches.

If a feudal lord somehow wins a political lottery in this land and finds himself ruling the country, he really treats the entire nation as his personal property. He, of course, never cares about the living conditions of his peasants. What he does care about is the annual return on the crops. That is precisely what peasants are for. They are meant to sweat and shed their blood so the feudal lord can have a greater profit. Now, who would argue against the feudal reasoning that the greater the size of the estate, the more will be its profits and hence the louder the expression of power that comes with it. It is, therefore, that Asif Ali Zardari has popularized the slogan of "Kaphey Kaphey Pakistan Kaphey" (Sindh wants to stay with Pakistan).

We have already seen how the country and its people suffer if it is an industrialist who has the steering wheel to himself. Who would dare to explain to an industrialist the simple fact that a nation is not a factory? A capitalist would have every incentive to replace hundreds of employees with new automated machines. Computers and machines are bound to reduce the expenses and increase the profit margin for the owner. But if the leader of a country imposes such policies in the name of downsizing and rightsizing, this would inevitably result in increased unemployment and hence higher levels of public unrest and anger. This contrasts with their normative role as leaders who are expected to create more employment opportunities for the citizenry so they can improve their lives standards. But again, we are talking about factory owners.

Now imagine what happens if an Islamist cleric somehow manages to establish his government (the mere imagination gives me goosebumps). They have already championed the art of corporal punishment as they have spent their lives using sticks and whips, forcing their disciples to memorize the lessons. They have zero tolerance for dissent as they declare people subscribing to sects and political parties other than their own as sinister and at-fault. They impose their

21

own interpretations of Islam and sharia and consider those who would dare to have a different opinion as infidels and liable to be killed. You do not expect them to compromise and accommodate others when they display boards outside their mosques which clearly warn the entrants: "People from other sects are not allowed to enter the premises of this mosque." Now imagine what a spiritually fulfilling environment we shall have under such leadership and what exemplary interfaith harmony we shall witness at the society level. Would that not be an ideal society? For now, just let the mixed bag of Islamist clerics reach some consensus on any interpretation of Islam, sharia, and equality.

When it comes to enforced solutions and authoritarian governance, we have had rich experiences under several impositions of military martial laws. Have they really helped? But as Iqbal had explained;

> *Jhapatna, palatna, palat kar jhapatna*
> *Lahu gar'm rakhney ka hai ik bahana*

The futile exercise of doing the same and expecting a different outcome has become a golden rule of our military bureaucracy: dig a trench and bury the dirt, dig another trench. You do not need to care about what you achieve as long as you look busy doing something. If it is not enough for you to do on the borders, there must be a plethora of work to do inside them. Frequently overthrowing the elected civilian government is one of them. After all, silencing the stupid civilians must be in the greater interests of the nation. What if you do not have the wherewithal to establish a direct military rule? There must be ways to work around it. All you have to do is to greedily protect your strategic assets. You need to keep them engaged so they are not out of form when required. And if in the process, some voiceless and wretched of the earth have to lose their lives, it is not a big deal. For great causes, there are always some trivial sacrifices you have to make. But, come on, have we, not all realized that these experiments have devastated the state and society?

We are surrounded by political leaders who have demarcated the country into territories exactly like the underworld mafia. If anyone mistakenly enters their territory, we frequently hear in the news, either they are target-killed, or their mutilated bodies are discovered in gunny sacks. Don't we come across such horrible news quite frequently? They prompt me to imagine what happens if one day an underworld don rises to rule this country. They will collect extortions instead of taxes and spy agencies will be tasked to 'field'. *Bhai Log*[1] will replace judges in the court proceedings and *parchis*[2] will serve as government notifications. Criminals will be punished only when the *supari*[3] is paid in full. Wouldn't that be wonderful? The citizenry would not suffer long-and indecisive court proceedings in search of justice- no more eternal wait

---

[1] a term used in urban India and Pakistan to refer to the gangsters

[2] a handwritten chit, a short note

[3] ransom amount

for a court decision. Perhaps the public and I shall have some peace when such a 'stationery bandit'[4] establishes his rule.

Let me tell you a story from my school time. In school, we would get bored to hell by the monotony of uninteresting subjects. We would desperately wait for that one period-a-week of entertainment which was set aside for physical training (PT). In that session, a retired Subadar[5] who had a whistle hanging by a thread around his neck would lead us to school ground. That whistle which we called *'ushpalaq'* in our mother tongue was a call of salvage to our bored souls. In the ground, we would run around shouting and screaming and enjoying ourselves. Since the physical training instructor (PTI) was a former military man, he would impose a strict discipline. Recalling his days in the army, he would often get nostalgic.

That memory has triggered my mind to imagine what state and society we would have if a disciplinarian sportsperson or a physical training instructor gets to govern this country. People would be running all around, shouting and screaming, having fun but without accomplishing much. That imagination is helped by the kind of statements issued by the opposition leader Imran Khan we are coming across these days. "I shall blow three wickets in a single go", "All I need is a decent team", "No one would stand my

---

[4]Mancur Olson, "Dictatorship, Democracy, and Development", American Political Science Review, Volume 87, No. 3, September 1993.

[5]a term used in Pakistan for military personnel which is higher than havildars and lower than lieutenants.

bowling", "We shall clean sweep next election (Howzat)." Where do people and their genuine issues stand in these sports-cum-political commentaries? Well, their role is limited to keep watching the match and keep on clapping. That is all they are for. Ahh, only if someone could explain to these young players that politics is not the same as sports and that a state is not a sports arena.

Can't our politicians simply take a state as a state is? Why do they have to treat it as their property, their factory, their madrassa, their territory, or their dressing room? Can this country withstand more experiments? Can we, as a public, ever expect a genuine leader governing the country who would consider herself/himself a representative of the people and answerable to the people a leader who treats the citizenry as the ultimate strength as well as the ultimate source of authority?

December 18, 2012

3

We are citizens of the country...

akistan is said to have been established in the name of Islam. Some, hence, call it "The Islamic Fort". There are narcissists who even romanticize the fact that ours is the only nuclear power within the Muslim world. Now the generous conferral of such a fantastic title must be creating a glorified image of Pakistan: a country where equality, justice, solidarity, brotherhood, and peace and security would be in abundance; the citizenry would be prosperous and none would starve, people would respect each other, and its enemies would tremble out of fear when thinking of Pakistan's prowess. One would imagine that Pakistan is an ideal country in every respect. But we all know that the reality is in stark contrast to such fantastic imagination.

In reality, we are residents of a country where, on the one hand, rulers have been fooling the citizenry in the name of religion and, on the other hand, the public

26

is also used to getting conned in the name of Islam. Bigotry is at display in our public attitudes. If someone avoids prosecution after committing a crime, he shamelessly 'thanks God'. Robbers who rob without getting caught, murderers who get away with murders, bureaucrats getting huge sums in bribe, food producers who make loads of money by tampering the rates of commodities with artificial shortage, even small business owners who evade taxes, or sex traffickers and drug mafia who keep running their businesses with impunity, all thank no one but Allah for their unhindered and uninterrupted income. Hallelujah! All praises to Allah.

We are residents of the country wherein a case of a deadly traffic accident or a natural calamity, the first arrivers frequently rob the diseased and the injured, stealing watches and jewellery instead of helping them. In the dear homeland of ours, strongholds of drug mafia and sex traffickers avoid surveillance of our security enforcement agencies but, ironically, we cannot perform religious rituals and offer prayers in our mosques, imambargahs, and other places of worship until and unless we have policemen and armed security personnel on guard. We live in a country where our compatriots are never tired of speaking out against human rights violations elsewhere but where they conveniently turn a blind eye to attacks, murders, and bombings taking place right in their city. We are citizens of a country where the judiciary issues sou motu notices to protect a love affair but forgets to take notice of daily attacks on

27

vulnerable social groups. The power dynamics are such that the whole society media put on trial an enticing but weak female actress for a nonissue such as the discovery of a bottle of wine from her luggage[1] but if a juggernaut proclaims live on television that not only, he drinks but also entertains full parties, we suddenly discover an appreciation for personal space and choices. In the dear country of ours, an elected prime minister can be removed from office for a statement interpreted as contempt of court[2] but where no one cares to punish murderous hate groups for insulting humans and humanity. Here, ruthless murderers roam freely,[3] and vulnerable individuals and communities are left to their mercy in appeasement. All these injustices constitute the daily affairs of our dear country which, it is said, was established in the name of Islam, which is the fort of Islam, and which is the sole nuclear power in the entire Islamic world.

We are citizens of a country where humanity bleeds and reality shamelessly laughs in the face of glorified fantasies.

January 3, 2013

---

[1]Pakistan Today, "SC takes notice of Odho's release", Pakistan Today, June 7, 2011,
https://archive.pakistantoday.com.pk/2011/06/07/sc-takes-notice-of-odho's-release/.

[2]DAWN News, "Yousaf Raza Gilani is sent packing", DAWN News, June 19, 2012,
https://www.dawn.com/news/727782.

[3]Geo TV, "دہشت گردوں کو بتانا چاہتا ہوں کہ ہم نے امن کا آغاز کیا ہے: مولانا الد عیانوی", Geo TV, March 14, 2014.

4

For what sins were we killed?

"Baba, who are these people who hate us enough to kill us every other day?" is the question that my perplexed daughter has asked me repeatedly. Upon her return from school, she is usually full of questions. One day, on her arrival she was particularly sad. After we had our lunch, when I asked, she told me that one of the two people who had been gunned down that day was her friend's father. They share the same ride to and from the school and that day on her way back home, her friend had cried all along.

"Father, why do they kill us?" she asked me the same question again. Understanding my inability to offer any solid explanation, she continued, "Today a classmate of mine asked me this very question?" "What did you say in response?" "I told her that our target-killers were simply jealous of us. They were scared of our passionate association with education and hard work and that they envied our social attitude towards

29

hygiene and cleanliness." As if she was not convinced of her own hypothesis, she continued, "But really, father, can our love for education, our inclination for earning our livelihood through wage labouring instead of choosing to beg and tidy surrounding be sins big enough to convince someone to kill us?"

As always, I stayed silent. How could I tell her that in this intolerant society of ours, our list of sins is really long and that each individual item in the long list is sufficient in its own right to warrant our death? Is this a trifling crime that in a society where the literacy rate is shamefully low, ours is a people who prioritize education and whose younger generation is a hundred percent literate? That could probably explain why students going to their schools, colleges, and universities are targeted.[1] But I could not express my mind and before I could articulate an answer, my daughter threw me another question, "Father, what harm could these poor laborers have done to anybody for they are frequently targeted?"[2] Ah, in a country where the ruling elite is used to begging for charity at the doors of international donors and where mismanagement and corruption by consecutive governments have pushed poor citizens to either beg on the streets or commit suicide, how can earning a piece of bread for one's family with integrity and

---

[1] Saleem Shahid, "Four dead, 72 hurt as bomb rips through university bus in Quetta", Dawn, June 19, 2012,   https://www.dawn.com/news/727679.

[2] Euan McKirdy and Sophia Saifi, "At least 20 killed in market blast in Pakistani city of Quetta", CNN, April 12, 2019, https://edition.cnn.com/2019/04/12/asia/quetta-market-blast-intl/index.html.

backbreaking labour be a pardonable crime? Only that could explain why the poorest of the poor blue-collar daily wagers are shot dead.[3] But today, my daughter's impatient mind was bursting with questions. Before I would respond, she asked again, "Is cleanliness a crime too? How can you frustrate someone by keeping your house and neighbourhood tidy?" I wished to explain to her that in a city where overflowing mounds of garbage are blocking the traffic, where the stench from the roadside waste makes one asphyxiate, and where the very individuals reciting the verse, "Cleanliness constitutes half of one's faith," are used to piling garbage out on the street isn't it a sin to tidy one's house and maintain one's streets? Doesn't that explain why Quetta's streets are bloodied with the blood of these innocents? I also wanted to tell her that the very teachers, intellectuals, and political leaders who strive to promote knowledge, fight hatred, and encourage love are all criminals. Only that could justify why they are silenced by bullets in their heads. I intended to tell my daughter that in this government of ours, all ministers and senior bureaucrats rush to hire 'their own men' as soon as there are new vacancies. And yet, they are careful enough to leave at least some jobs for us, the resourceless candidates whose only hopes are their education and skills. This is so that their ministries and offices have at least some talented individuals who can keep the system from crumbling

[3]Peggy Bruguiere, "Pakistani extremists film massacre of Shiite minority group", France 24, 07/02/2012,
https://observers.france24.com/en/20120702-pakistan-quetta-extremists-film-massacre-shiite-minority-group-hazara.

down in a total disaster. Now, in a system where no one is taking ownership, if these few talented individuals start working even harder, more than they ought to, isn't that a crime in itself? Isn't that why Hazara government officials are target-killed.[4] But again, before I could tell this, she threw me another question, "I have heard that our ancestors and youngsters have served Pakistan really well. Many have sacrificed their lives, especially in the military. Didn't General Musa defend the nation in 1965? Our teacher tells us that our forefathers served Pakistan in every field. Why, then, would our Pakistani brothers kill us? Is this the reward we get in return for our patriotism?" To this question, I did not have any answer except a plain admission: yes, patriotism too must be one in the long list of our crimes.

I was struggling to explain to her that our biggest of all crime is being a numerical minority. If all people are put into boxes based on their beliefs, languages, cultures, we would make a tiny box and that indeed is our biggest and most unforgivable crime. I wished to muster up the courage and tell my daughter once and for all that, in the eyes of our killers, even our mothers, our aged, and our children were all criminals because they were all Hazara. In the eyes of our murderers, our mere existence was a crime. Wasn't that why passenger buses were stopped at gunpoint, Hazara passengers were singled out, lined-up, and shot?[5]

---

[4] Human Rights Watch, "We are the Walking Dead", Human Rights Watch, June 29, 2014,

[5] Shezad Baloch, "Sectarian atrocity: 29 killed in Mastung, Quetta ambushes", Express Tribune, September 20, 2011,
https://tribune.com.pk/story/256419/gunmen-attack-bus-in-balochistan-20-killed.

Today, I wished to tell my daughter everything once and for all. I wanted to tell her that we had always been serving Pakistan with full devotion and patriotism, and with the firm belief that this was the land we would always call home. That we had always gone an extra mile to serve this society and prove our loyalty. But alas... rather than putting our murderers behind bars, our rulers mock us[6] by promising to send us a truckload of tissue papers[7] so we can wipe off our tears.[8] Some of our compatriots have fixated their eyes on our properties and businesses and others are not even trying to conceal their schadenfreude. Our fellow citizenry? Well, they are busy thanking God that the fire has broken only in the neighbourhood and that they are Alhamdulillah safe in their houses. And our murderers? They must be angels or super magicians because they are just invisible to our law enforcement agencies.

I mustered up all the courage left in me to tell all this to my young daughter. But then she had already fallen asleep. Perhaps she did not expect any

[6]Shar, "Hazaras, The Rohingyas of Pakistan?", Express Tribune, November 2, 2017,

https://tribune.com.pk/article/59433/hazaras-the-rohingyas-of-pakistan.

[7]Haider Changezi, "Chief Minister Balochistan Mocks Hazara Killings", Hazara News Pakistan, October 5, 2011,

https://hazaranewspakistan.wordpress.com/2011/10/05/chief-minister-balochistan-mocks-hazara-killings/.

[8]Saleem Javed, "With the Raisani government gone, will the Hazara killings stop?", Dawn, January 30, 2013,
https://www.dawn.com/news/782401.

explanation from me. Or maybe she had realized her questions did not have easy answers.

January 11, 2013

This article was written a day after the twin bombing of Alamdar Road which killed 115 people, injuring more than 200.

5

Why do we forget ...?

As soon as we start arguing about religious or political beliefs, why do we suddenly forget our otherwise accommodating behaviour, our appreciation for a broader vision, our usually careful attitude to navigate through delicate affairs, and instead we resort to verbal abuse and adrenaline rush for a fistfight? This is particularly interesting because we seem to be quite accommodating in most other affairs on an everyday basis. Just look around. You will come across a rich variety in people's choices for dressing, moustache and hairstyle, shoe preferences, selection of perfumes, their sense of beauty to decorate their cars, or different genres of the melodious music coming out of their vehicles. Have you ever seen someone who would argue and behead someone merely because the other person was wearing a different coloured dress or having a different hairstyle or was listening to Ustad Sarahang instead of Muhammad Rafi? No, you wouldn't. We all overlook these differences and treat them as personal choices and individual preferences.

It is not only the above. Does everyone have the same choice when it comes to food? Don't we choose our careers and businesses at our convenience and our passion? We might even disagree with a lot that happens in the name of fashion and societal norms, especially rituals around weddings, but we don't attack the families with weapons. Of course, not. We remind ourselves, it's their choice and their affair. We might prefer to send our children to missionary schools or to schools where they attend Islamic courses too. We do have differences of opinion on these, but it does not get to a fistfight. But as soon as we discuss religious or political ideologies, we seem to forget all about the art of effective communication, the norms and etiquettes of dialogue and, we find ourselves verbally abusing each other or even worse, engaged in physical violence. We seem to forget that faith and beliefs are also matters of personal choice. Everyone considers themselves answerable to God in their way. Every human is entitled to choose and perform their religious beliefs and rituals with complete liberty and without any pressure or compulsion. But we lose all our rationality when it comes to religious and political beliefs and identities. We turn ourselves deaf and blind and we tolerate nothing different from us.

This is a classic case of narcissism when one firmly believes he is right and all but him are misguided. This is where the conflict begins. We do not hesitate to judge and issue fatwa as soon as we come across an opinion which is different from ours. We then become ambitious to make everyone believe in what we believe is right. However, we do not engage with such a level of God-fearing religiosity when children of our poor neighbours are starving, or if someone is dying because she/he cannot afford medical expenses, or when a widow is struggling to put food on the table for her children. In these cases, we satisfy our religious zeal by being grateful to Allah for what we have to ourselves (without having to share it) and for patronizing those poor souls to be grateful to the Lord in all events. We are undoubtedly reluctant to help these deserving souls around us in private. It is a different matter altogether if we can generously give away alms (Sadaqat) and charity (Khairaat) in public to display how God-fearing and generous donators we are!

When we are debating different religions, we reduce the people from all other faiths to mere infidels. But if we are debating various sects within Islam, even Muslims from all other sects seem infidels to us. And worst of all, a group within a sect does not feel like sharing a table with another group from the same sect with a slight difference of opinion. How many of us can comfortably pray in a mosque of a different sect? Have we not so passionately striven to guide others to our imagined paradise that we have often created a hell out of this tangible world of ours? Although all religions and faiths preach love and humanity, ironically, we forget all about love and humanity as we start debating religions. We violate all the moral and legal codes and resort to resolving all affairs with brute force and violence.

Around the world, states legislate to maintain law and order. Societies, around the globe, have their moral norms which in combination with state laws, maintain peace and order. The legal and moral codes define what rights and responsibilities individuals have. As goes a famous saying, "Your liberty to swing your arm ends where my nose begins." When tolerance and compassion die in a society and the institutions, social groups, and individuals violate their constitutional boundaries, it is bound to slide into chaos and anarchy.

It is one of the great misfortunes of Pakistan that not only institutions, but also social groups and individuals have all started to overstep their constitutional boundaries. As a result, the situation in the country is getting worsened and there have been serious questions raised over its stability in the long run. If we aspire to establish a civil and peaceful society, we will need to respect other individuals' and communities' right to belief or none thereof. But then again, as soon as we are debating religious and political beliefs, why do we suddenly forget all our etiquettes, our lessons for effective communication, our appreciation for a broader vision, our accommodating behaviour, and our care for humanity, and we find ourselves engaged in verbal abuse, physical violence or even worse, terrorism?

January 30, 2013

6

Social Media or Public Toilet?

We all know how advancements in technology and the resulting revolution in communications have transformed our world into a global village. But as we appreciate the overwhelming variety of communication platforms, let us not forget about the most inexpensive or rather free platform: public toilets, where you get exposed to random thoughts through a variety of expressions from calligraphy to abstract art. These art pieces tell us a lot about the mentality of their creators. And even better, through these free art displays, you could get a glimpse of where the society stands.

Let's imagine, you are on your daily walk strolling at a good distance from home or running errands and you feel some unfriendly motion in your stomach. Initially, you would try to ignore it but soon you realize this is getting serious and that you will not be able to contain it for too long. At a certain level of realization, you forget all about your lined-up meetings, the shopping bags in your hands, or other affairs and suspiciously start looking around. There is a good crowd around you. If it was just a minor affair and you were not under the surveillance of so many eyeballs, you would have dared to get yourself a corner to attend to nature's call. But that's out of the question now. You desperately push your brain to recall the whole urban map of your surroundings and just then, you remember there used to be a public toilet in the third street from where you are standing. Your mind starts emergency navigation, following the shortest path to the destination while hoping the public toilet is still there. As you are approaching the much-desired destination, you realize the storm in your stomach is also getting stronger than ever. Your eyes brighten up at the sight of the desperately needed toilet. Ahh... thank God, it is not overcrowded. You get in and after you partially relieve yourself and as you resume breathing again, you realize you are drenched in sweat. You take out your handkerchief and wipe the sweat off your forehead. And there, precisely at that moment, your eyes catch a sight of the great canvas that the toilet door is offering, housing a whole lot of text and pictorial art pieces. Your eyeballs roll to the right and left and find that the walls are no less than a museum. You come across a wide variety of slogans; "Death to ABC" and "Long live XYZ" along with explicitly sexual poetry and pornographic drawings pointing to someone's attempt at creating masterpieces. Some of these marvellous drawings have been sketched with pencils, some with coal, and others are carved with the tip of a knife. Then you see some sort of a vague text attempted in weird suspicious colours and you realize some creative ones must have dipped their fingers in their heart blood to express their rich emotions they must have been overwhelmed with. Who knows who these legendary minds are behind such masterpieces? The public toilet artists did not sign their art pieces and did not disclose their identities. All they did was to relieve themselves and release their frustration along and leave anonymously.

Anyway, public toilets are certainly one platform where everyone can express whatever ideas they have without disclosing their identities and without giving a damn about the consequences. Many people who could not express themselves otherwise, use that venue to take out their frustration. But then many people develop a habit of anonymously expressing their indecent thoughts without an ounce of accountability. Many people use social media for precisely the same thing. Take Facebook, for example. Most people use Facebook to connect and communicate with family members and friends (which is what this platform was designed for in the first place). Still, many use this platform just as a public toilet with unrestrained verbal abuse, political sloganeering, harassing people, issuing threats, spreading rumours, promoting made-up stories, and creating unnecessary suspense. Don't you come across such nonsense?

Some Juma Khan* would be running a fake account in the name of Shah Rukh Khan, some random Abdul Wadood* would be posting stuff as Waheed Murad and a Khuda Bukhsh* as Saif Ali Khan. Some Adam Khan* would cover up as Katrina Kaif and Ghulam Sakhi as Madhuri would appear in every group conversation, abuse their political rivals and get away without taking any responsibility for their comments. Some friends of mine who have been personally offended by these fake account users call these anonymous abusers the "Cyber Target-killers." They mask their face, hide their identity, wait in the dark to ambush their political opponents, and attack them with criticism, curses, and even harassment and threats. The weirdly scary part is that you might even have normal relationships with these toxic individuals in real life and you might have shared dining tables on more than one occasion. They are just used to leading dual lives and do not want to abandon the comfort of expressing themselves with zero sense of responsibility.

Restrictions on freedom of expression in developing societies are a major factor behind such deviating behaviours. Therefore, many individuals take out their frustrations in this way. But they seem to forget that social media is a public space accessible to anyone. Anybody could judge our society and its weaknesses and cleavages. We should remember that we cannot effectively communicate our point of view through abuse and uncivil exchange. Instead, such inhumane interaction exchange only adds to our frustrations, hate levels, and chaos in the society which we already have in abundance.

The original article was first published on DAWN Urdu website on February 09, 2013.[1]

DAWN Urdu, "پبلک ٹوائلٹ ", February 09, 2013, https://www.dawnnews.tv/news/59986/social-network-or-public-toilet-aq.

7

We are not alone in this!

The discussion was at its climax. This young group of friends had come to the picnic spot at the foot of the mountain, a little distant from their neighbourhood. Comfortable on their picnic rug and sipping tea in unending cycles, they were engaged in a never-ending debate instead of enjoying themselves with ludo, cards, and music. Their voices would intermittently get louder. Sometimes, many of them would speak at once. It seemed everyone was passionate to be heard before all others.

"Look, I still insist that it is our religious identity as a Shia that can explain why we are killed," said a boy with a neatly trimmed beard. "When they claim responsibility, don't they mention our Shia identity to justify their acts of terrorism?", he continued. "Don't we know who these guys are? They want to impose their version of sharia not only over Pakistan but across the region. In addition, they are not without collaborators.

43

Various internal and external actors are helping them out in this campaign. That explains why we do not get to witness any serious attempts at controlling these sectarian jihadis? But are we the only people in Pakistan who are obstructing their holy campaign?"

"I do not agree with you," protested a young man seated next to him. "It is not as simple as you would wish to think. I believe there are other strategic calculations behind the apparent cover of sectarianism. Balochistan, including our hometown Quetta, did not have a religious or a sectarian conflict as late as 15 years ago. But, today, the whole city has been held hostage by a bunch of terrorists. Meanwhile, we do not hear any news of violent sectarian conflicts in the Punjab province anymore. Although it was there that all this sectarian threat started in the 1990s. Even Khyber Pakhtunkhwa, Sindh and Kashmir are far better than Balochistan, particularly Quetta, in terms of sectarian harmony. This is strange because there are larger Shia communities out of Balochistan but somehow, they do not receive the amount and the degree of violence we do here. I believe this has something to do with Balochistan. Given its strategically important location and immense natural resources, many international powers have fixated their eyes on this resource-rich but poorly governed region. These international actors see their future economic interests pinned to this region and so they want an unstable security situation in Balochistan to ward off their competing investors. But then again, the question is why specifically the Hazaras are targeted to accomplish these large strategic projects?"

"You are entitled to your opinion, my friends, but I firmly believe our killings have a lot to do with our local business competitors who want to throw us out of the market," argued the young trader who was keen to pitch his hypothesis. "You guys are too political whereas this battle is purely for economic gains. Quetta is the capital of Pakistan's largest province and serves as the only trade hub in this vast region. Balochistan shares borders with Iran and Afghanistan and trade with these countries can happen only through Quetta. Not only do people come from towns and villages around Quetta but also a large number of traders converge here. We, the Hazaras, have been an important actor in the local trades and businesses and there are rogue groups who want to terrorize us and push us out of the market. They want to capture our prime businesses and estates in the city."

"I absolutely disagree with you," said a young man who had been patiently listening until then. "Insecurity, targeted-killings, and bomb explosions have affected every class of traders in Quetta. People from other provinces have ceased to converge here. This is worrisome for everybody. I think Saudi Arabia and Iran are fighting a proxy war at the cost of our lives and businesses. These two arrogant regional powers have tall claims to leadership of the Muslim world, and they are keen to dominate one another and establish their hegemony in the region. These two oil-rich nations are spending extravagantly to earn passionate supporters in this region and to suppress their opposition by brute force. Neither of these two so called leaders of the Muslim world has the wherewithal to pin down non-Muslim powers yet they are busy calling out each other. As far as we are concerned, it is pure misfortune that, against our wishes, we shall be used as fuel in this proxy war. Perhaps the predators are specifically choosing us because we are an easy prey. They can achieve their objective, and nobody will even hear our frantic cries."

"We are missing out something here, "said another young man with an intellectual look. "There is no peace in any corner of Pakistan as we speak. Daily death toll in Karachi is as high as a dozen. Some of them fall prey to sectarian violence, others to ethnic and political clashes. Look at Khyber Pakhtunkhwa: bomb blasts, attacks on public offices and places of worship are routine there. Even if you do not see violent sectarian conflict in the Punjab, security officers and personnel of law enforcement agencies are still targeted infrequently. Gilgit, Parachinar, and the tribal areas are ablaze in the fire of terrorism. When it comes to Balochistan, is there anyone who feels safe and secure? On the one hand, there are people murdered by the secessionist Baloch forces for suspicion of being government informants. On the other hand, every other day, mutilated bodies of Baloch nationalists are recovered from across the province. Innocent members of the settler communities and Pashtuns are not spared either. Religious leaders from all communities are being targeted as well. Our genocide is an open book. I fully believe that all this is due to the evil forces who have identified fault lines in our society, and they are exploiting these divisions to weaken Pakistan. Eventually, they wish to erase Pakistan altogether from the map of the globe."

"What if our murderers are wreaking havoc to weaken the federal government's grip on Balochistan so that ultimately Balochistan could be freed from Pakistan?" contributed another youngster. "Or perhaps the very opposite: ultra-patriotic forces may be killing us to give an impression to the international community that Balochistan's real conflict is sectarian in nature and not nationalistic. They can use our murder to divert attention from Balochistan's historical conflict with the centre. Outside the country, wherever the situation in Pakistan is discussed Hazara genocide is a huge issue these days. But again, the same question: why specifically us?"

As soon as there was a brief break in their arguments, one of them who was busy cooking for them also joined the group back. From his facial features, he seemed a reckless youngster who would rarely get into serious political debates. And yet at this moment, he did have something to say.

"There will be some time before the meal is ready," everyone listened to him. Realising that he has earned everybody's attention, he continued, "I have been listening to your arguments all the while. I am not as educated as you guys are. I don't read as many books as you guys do. I don't even know how to operate a computer or navigate through the internet. At most, I watch TV sometimes or read some newspapers. I

47

cannot articulate as well as you all do but I do feel the pain. I have no idea who is killing us and why. I want to fight back but who should I fight? What I know for certain is that hundreds of our young, old, children and women have been murdered during the last 13 years. Thousands of people have been injured in these attacks and hundreds of them have become permanently disabled. Countless children have lost their fathers and women their husbands. Yes, we have been attacked while praying in our imambargahs and mosques but also on the roads. Our labourers have been ambushed and our students have been killed. Government employees from our community have been target-killed and traders have been sprayed with bullets. Nobody is safe. For me it is not important if we are being massacred because we are seen as Shia or Hazara. For me it is enough that we are being killed. We are specifically singled out, lined up, and killed. There is not a single Hazara in Quetta who has not lost a brother, a friend or a relative in this genocidal wave of terrorism. Are we the only Shias in Balochistan? Even in other towns of Balochistan, why are they specifically going after the Hazaras? Hazara families had been living in Mach and Khuzdar for generations. They speak local languages in these areas just as their mother tongue. What baffles me is that not a single killer or a terrorist has been arrested to this day. How can a target-killer spray bullets right in front of the police and Frontier Corps check posts and yet escape unharmed? Nobody cares to chase them. After hundreds of attacks on Hazara community, our government has failed to capture a single terrorist as if these terrorists landed from the skies and flew back to heavens after cold-bloodedly killing our community members. Perhaps these terrorists are so powerful that nobody in the government dares to go after them. Even our fellow citizens and neighbours are turning a blind eye to our tragedy. They see our blood in their streets and yet do not break their silence? I wonder if somebody can be forced to give up their religious beliefs or if somebody's ethnic identity can be forcefully erased? If some groups somewhere think they can turn Quetta into a prison for us where we shall be massacred and nobody will even notice our genocide, they are at fault. But there is hope. Look out, there are people from all faiths marching on the streets not only across Pakistan but across the globe as well. They are amplifying and echoing our calls for justice. They are out there in solidarity to tell us that we are not alone in this. They are marching to tell us that we are not weak. They are protesting to send us a message: humanity is still alive. As long as humanity is alive, nobody can eliminate us."

Thus, he finished his talk and rose up. Silence ruled their assembly for a while. Gradually, they all rose up to eat the meal that was ready.

February 16, 2013.

49

8

You are welcome but late

On Saturday, February 16, Quetta was bathed in Hazara blood again..[1] It was for the first-time many people came to know about C-4, an explosive chemical. This liquid explosive killed more than 90 people including children and women. The explosion was so devastating that more than a dozen people just disappeared into thin air. Nobody found any traces of their bodies.

A few weeks earlier, on January 10, when the rest of the world was still celebrating the arrival of the new year, Lashkar-e-Jhangavi (LeJ) killed over a hundred people in a twin explosion on Alamdar Road.[2] We were gifted with the dead bodies of our dear ones on the occasion of the new year. In the aftermath of the Alamdar Road bombings, nonviolent protests within and beyond Pakistan resulted in dissolution of the

---

[1] BBC, "Pakistan: Dozens dead in bomb attack on Quetta market", BBC, February 17, 2013, https://www.bbc.com/news/world-asia-21485731.

[2] BBC, "Pakistan blasts: Scores killed at Quetta snooker hall", BBC, January 10, 2013, https://www.bbc.com/news/world-asia-20969443.

Raisani's provincial cabinet.[3] Governor Zulfiqar Magsi imposed governor rule as demanded by the protestors. This act by the government, somehow, managed to alleviate the pains and wounds of the Hazara community. But they miserably failed us again. Despite high level political reshuffling, Quetta's citizens failed to witness any improvements in the law-and-order situation. Frontier Corps were already deployed in the city, and they had full policing authority. And yet, Quetta never ceased to bleed. Protestors had demanded a targeted operation against the sectarian terrorists but that never happened. Many critical observers point to the discrepancies as whatever operations were conducted, they targeted Baloch ethno-nationalists instead of sectarian terrorists of the Lashkar-e-Jhangavi. Citizens of Balochistan in general and members of the Hazara community in particular, desperately waited for some news of relief. And what happened next? Almost a month since the Alamdar Road explosions, even a bigger explosion rocked the other Hazara neighbourhood of the Hazara Town. It was a well-understood fact that the terrorists would not take easy the dissolution of a corrupt government particularly where certain members were not only benefitting from a partnership with these thugs but also protecting these mafias. It was certain that they would do everything to sabotage the imposed governor's rule. And so, Quetta was bathed in the blood of innocent children, women, and the aged and the young of Hazara community. But what baffles everyone

---

[3]"بلوچستان میں عملی طور پر گورنر راج نافذ", DAWN, January 14, 2013, https://www.dawnnews.tv/news/51556/chief-minister-balochistan-agrees-to-resign.

alike is how a thousand kilogram of this highly sophisticated and lethal explosive liquid chemical passed through the series of security checkpoints to arrive and wreak havoc at the heart of the Hazara Town. Residents of this ill-fated city know very well what an ordinary citizen has to go through at each of these checkpoints. Even individuals who keep licensed pistols for their personal safety undergo harsh questioning. Under predictable security threats and amongst these many security checkpoints, how then a vehicle with such a volume of highly lethal explosive could easily pass through without being detected and reach its target location? Indeed, this solidifies the suspicion that there must be some collaborators and facilitators of terrorists within the security apparatus.

What has been observed as a repeated pattern in previous attacks on the Hazara community within and outside Quetta is that the law enforcement agencies did not care to chase the target-killers. This despite the fact that many of these terrorist incidents took place in close proximity to the checkpoints manned by the Frontier Corps or the Balochistan police. In some cases, as many as dozens of people were butchered right between two checkpoints near each other. The government still owes us an explanation for the gruesome incident in September 2011 when a passenger bus was stopped, all passengers were identified and the Hazara members were singled out, lined up and shot dead.[4] Nobody has yet explained who

---

[4] Shezad Baloch, "Sectarian atrocity: 29 killed in Mastung, Quetta ambushes", Express Tribune, September 20, 2011,
https://tribune.com.pk/story/256419/gunmen-attack-bus-in-balochistan-20-killed.

blocked the traffic on the busy highway on both sides for more than 30 minutes while the terrorists were busy identifying, lining up and shooting the Hazara passengers. All this happened right in the native constituency of our chief minister in Mastung, and still no explanations? People still inquire who was behind the suicide attack at the residence of the powerful minister from Chagai district? Why were proper investigations not conducted and why has somebody not taken notice of the incident? If there was transparency in our affairs and we had answers to all these questions, we would be in a better position to solve the mystery that the Hazara genocide has become. But there is little we can hope for when there are still people at the helm of affairs who care the least for us and who are still busy stitching ridiculous excuses for their inaction. Take Ayatollah Durrani for instance, the elected member of the national assembly from the ruling Pakistan Peoples' Party (PPP), who coined a new joke on a live TV program: "The Hazaras kill each other so they could claim asylum in Australia." And there are still others who are trying really hard to put the blame for our massacres on the Baloch nationalists so that the real killers could be protected.

Members of the Hazara community and other peace-loving constituents of Balochistan have long been demanding a crackdown against the sectarian terrorists. There has been a real demand for destroying the hideouts and safe havens of these violent extremist groups. People want their patrons and collaborators to be unmasked. But all these cries for transparency and justice have gone in vain and we see a rise in the frequency and scale of violence against the vulnerable Hazara community. It is not selective killings anymore. Terrorists are attacking the Hazaras randomly with no regard for gender or age of the victims.

After the January explosions on Alamdar Road, the way the bereaved families protested was unique in Pakistan's history. In below freezing temperatures, they simply sat on Alamdar Road with coffins and refused to bury their dead for more than four days. They rejected normalization of the terrorist attacks on them and burials as routine. This peaceful, symbolic and yet very powerful gesture shook the conscience of thousands in Pakistan and people took to the streets in all major cities in expression of solidarity. The inefficient provincial cabinet was finally dissolved. What is important, however, is that there was still no action taken against the 'strategic assets' who are the real culprits behind this row of genocidal violence. We did not have to wait long to see the consequence for this inaction. The massacre on February 16 stands as a grim reminder.

Yet again, the government machinery seems to have initiated a targeted operation against the sectarian terrorists. Yet again, there are deep doubts about how serious the decision-makers really are. Are they just trying to pacify the protesting Hazara community? Shall we one day see the terrorist masterminds in the court of justice or shall they escape the 'high-security prisons'[5] yet again? Even if the

[5]The News International, "Usman Kurd, the man who caused the fall of Raisani government", The News International, January 15, 2013, https://www.thenews.com.pk/archive/print/627907-usman-kurd,-the-man-who-caused-fall-of-raisani-govt.

security establishment is serious in its current operation, I wonder why they hesitated to take any action earlier? Was it necessary for them to wait and witness as thousands of precious lives were lost at the hands of the violent extremists? Did they really need to wait for pieces of our children and our loved ones torn apart to trigger their conscience? Shall our children be able to attend schools and universities without any threats? Can our mothers feed and nourish our babies with the confidence that they will never have to collect their flesh and bones in plastic bags once they are old enough to walk out on the streets?

Honourable Chief Justice, together with these security institutions whom we entrust with our lives, may I register that even you are really late to take a Suo motu notice for innocent people have long been killed without any accountability. But then what else can we do but welcome any step in the right direction however late and however little that may be, as a line of Urdu poetry reads;

Deyr lagi aaney mein tum ko, Shuk'r hai phir bhi aaye tou

(You are too late, my beloved, but I can only be grateful you actually did come)

This piece was carried by DAWN Urdu on February 23, 2013, after a week since the Hazara Town explosion.

9

An Open Letter to Pakistan

To,

The Islamic Republic of Pakistan

Your Excellency,

I am an ordinary Pakistani, one of the 222 million who live across the length and breadth of Pakistan. Since I am a resident of Quetta, I will restrict this letter to Quetta. For a more precise introduction, I am one of those butchered on a daily basis; one of those murdered as a routine; my throat slit open merely to scare someone away; and my blood is spilled just to appease someone else. When your brotherly Muslim countries opt for the sectarian cold war, I bear the brunt of their proxy wars. It is my body that is torn into pieces by warring groups, and it is me who collect the body parts of my loved ones for burial. It is my house that gets set on fire for an excuse needed to halt elections, and it is my flesh and bones that build the strategist dreams of a new Balochistan. I should be grateful for I am the sacrificed for these noble causes.

After all, if my blood can appease brotherly Muslim countries and help the cause of collecting some charity, I should not complain. If my blood can serve as a pretext to launch military operations and save Balochistan from the Baloch, I should not complain. I do not even detest your patronized and protected strategic assets who are executing these megaprojects with such diligence. I can see their faces even behind many covers, but I would not complain because then they are diligently serving and saving the country and Islam. I believe they do not intend to really cleanse Pakistan off us. I believe they only want us, the enemies of Pakistan, to learn a lesson in patriotism. There is cause for celebration for they have succeeded in their holy mission, and their holy jihad has been gifting us with many more graves. And the more graves we dig for our loved ones, the more we learn how to love Pakistan. Such a beautiful relationship and such important lessons for us, the anti-state elements.

It does not frustrate me anymore that our murderers proactively proclaim responsibility for our massacres. I am writing this to express my gratitude for the few statements that your institutions have issued to condole. After your flag flew half-mast after the massacre of·hundreds of my community members, what more should I expect?

My beloved homeland,

I have always trusted your institutions. I do realize you have so many commitments. After all, you are the sole nuclear power of the Muslim world and as a good neighbour, you have additional responsibility on your burdened shoulders to protect the sovereignty of your fellow Muslim brother, Afghanistan. As the fort of Islam, you have to constantly stay alert and ward off threats to Islam. I am most certain Islam would be in great danger if something happened to you. Therefore, I don't believe a word of the reports from the anti-Islam and anti-state groups such as the Human Rights Commission of Pakistan (HRCP) and the Human Rights Watch (HRW) that question your sacred institutions and hold them to account for our massacres. I absolutely agree with you in that the human rights watchdogs are all foreign tools and serve the Jewish lobby to destabilize Pakistan. I totally agree with the spokesperson for the armed forces who recently said that the human rights groups in Pakistan are a tool in the hands of enemies and that their reports can exacerbate the sectarian harmony. He must be so right because he cannot be wrong. Ever. I also believed the director general (DG) of the Inter-Services Public Relations (ISPR) when he said all terrorists in Quetta could be traced back to two madrassas and that it was not difficult for the military to handle them only if the government requested them to step in.

I think international media are part of the conspiracy against Pakistan because they keep publishing reports about our mass killings. True it is that I am massacred but then publishing about these massacres would earn Pakistan a bad image. Don't you think so? I do not trust the ill-wishers of Pakistan when they say that even an ordinary police sepoy knows about these so-called terrorists, their whereabouts, their family connections, who protects them or even the details of their motorcycles and other vehicles. On the contrary, I completely believe the governor of Balochistan who, with utmost honesty and sincerity, announced a reward of 10 million rupees for anyone who shares information about these mysterious unknown assailants. I genuinely believe the administration will never reveal the identity of the informers just as the identity of these very terrorists has never been revealed.

I totally realize that the whole world is conspiring against Islam and, especially, against Pakistan. The United States, Israel, and India, in particular, are obsessed with Pakistan, I know. They cannot digest the fact that Pakistan rose to become a nuclear power despite poverty, unemployment, illiteracy, and political instability. Actually, they have no idea about our power of faith and our strength in passion. They do not know we can starve to death, but we shall not allow our enemies to even look us in the eye. Let me clarify, however, that when I use the term 'enemies', it does not apply to groups who are bombing and target-killing sinister minority communities like mine. These people are our very own assets and we have made a lot of efforts to train and groom them. They are heroically fighting our wars abroad and if our spoilt children create some mess at home, pardoning them should not be a big deal.

Your Highness,

Since I am a patriotic Pakistani and a faithful Muslim, I can sacrifice myself, my family, and my community for your larger interests, I actually want to thank you and your institutions for you have taken timely initiatives to protect us. I cannot forget the great favour you bestowed upon us when after we buried 1300 of our loved ones, you took immediate notice of the sufferings of our widows and orphans and killed a few of the terrorists in police encounters and arrested a few others in suspicion. I have believed you when you asked me not to worry anymore. I am thoroughly convinced that our protectors are still in full control of the affairs and that no one can harm us.

Your Excellency,

For the last few years, your intelligent agencies have commenced construction of security walls around us. These walls segregate us from the other residents of our city, but I am on the same page as your intelligent officers that these walls create a sense of safety in us. Even better, I think these walls with barbed wires, piled-up sandbags, and alert soldiers with visible weapons actually add much to the aesthetics of the city. Even our neighbours would have breathed a sigh of relief after these walls were erected. I can understand they had got bored with our sobbing and moaning. Finally, they won't have to tuck cotton buds into their ears so they could sleep peacefully. Even our children won't be able to wander away from home and play with the children of our neighbours. No hide and seek and no noise at all. Even I do not have to make up excuses to avoid attending wedding ceremonies of our neighbours because they are not our neighbours anymore. This super intelligent idea of segregating us from our neighbours in order to protect us from the threats we pose to each other is just mind-blowing and in compliance with sharia. I agree with your policymakers that it is easy to protect a community of hundreds of thousands by ghettoizing them in strictly guarded enclaves. The alternative involves going after the bunch of masterminds and busting terrorist cells, but it requires much more effort.

Pakistan has always been the "Fort of Islam", but your consecutive rulers have pursued amazing strategic policies and as a result, we can see the whole country is merely a large set of enclaves and forts. Some areas have been cordoned off with containers and declared as red zone and some others have been demarcated with security walls and checkouts and marked as 'sensitive'. Our rulers have a long tradition of enclosing themselves in fort like enclaves but now the citizenry is divided into gated closed communities as well. Please do not take me wrong. I am not against these well thought out measures taken for the protection of the common men and our rulers. I do not agree with anti-state conspiracy theorists who think these measures will create divisions in the long term. In fact, by writing this letter, I urge you to strictly instruct all your bureaucrats, generals, and policymakers to never give up pursuing these policies. Through this letter, I express my utmost respect and appreciation for the great services that our patriotic institutions and for the wisdom of our federal and provincial cabinets, especially our visionary, and truthful interior minister. It is only with the religious pursuit of these ambitious strategic policies that we can achieve the paradise-like Pakistan founded by its founder Muhammad Ali Jinnah and dreamt by the poet of the East, Allama Muhammad Iqbal.

I hope you will receive this letter with a degree of sympathy and consider the urges I have made. I shall remain grateful as always.

Yours obediently,
A Pakistani
Address: Alamdar Road Quetta, Pakistan

March 9, 2013

Note: This is a piece of satire.

IO

Or perish together as fools

As the rescuers and the victims of a suicide attack on the Sardar Bahadur Khan Women University's bus arrived at the Bolan Medical Complex, a second suicide bomber was waiting for them. The second attack was accompanied by further firing.[1] The ensuing shootout created chaos and mayhem. As the crew from the multiple TV channels had arrived to cover the initial attack, they started providing live commentary as gunshots were heard in the background during the second attack. Sensationalists as the media reporters are, they seemed eager to capitalize on this 'hot issue'. The pundits on the talk shows seemed equally energetic for they had such a lively issue at hand after some time. Commentators had a mayday. In particular the politicians from Balochistan, otherwise mostly

---

[1]BBC Urdu, " میں نے دیکھا کہ لوگوں کو گولیاں لگ رہی ہیں ", BBC Urdu, June 15, 2013, https://www.bbc.com/urdu/pakistan/2013/06/130615_eyewitness_accounts_sa.

ignored, seemed excited for the screen time they were getting. They were receiving multiple calls from various TV channels that needed their views and comments. TV channels were in stiff competition for the ratings. All this, while the police and the frontier corps were battling the deadly terrorists on the premises of the Bolan Medical Complex. Even the police and eyewitnesses were still not certain who the assailants were and why they had targeted these female students and yet, there were some speculators on the TV screen who were sharing their definite opinions with high degrees of confidence. It seemed as if these pundits were personally present at the planning meeting of the terrorists.

The first reckless statement came from Mir Hasil Bizenjo, the Vice President of the ruling National Party. Appearing on a TV channel, he confidently claimed the attack was intended at the female students from the Hazara community but that the terrorists had "unfortunately" hit the wrong bus. Sounding like a person who knows the inside story, he explained the attackers had targeted the wrong bus because the bus route for the Hazara students had recently been changed (as a matter of fact, the route had not been changed. The van for Hazara neighbourhood had mechanical faults). Hasil Bizenjo also claimed the terrorists had entered the Bolan Medical Complex in an ambulance, although the police seemed to have no clue. Such reckless commentary from Bizenjo surprised many. Some believe he added sensation to the story to divert attention from the latest attacks on Quaid-e

Azam Muhammad Ali Jinnah's residency in Ziarat which was claimed by the Baloch separatists, and which posed a major challenge to National Party and came as a shock to Dr. Malik who was optimistic about entering negotiations with the separatists. Clearly, he intended to cover up for his government's security loopholes by victim bashing.

The next day, I accidentally happened to watch a repeat telecast of a talk show which was initially broadcast when the gun battle at the Bolan Medical Complex was going on. The major point of debate was whether the attack was aimed at the Hazara students and whether the victims included Hazaras. Nawab Lashkari Raisani, former senator and elder brother to the former notorious Chief Minister Aslam Raisani, was among the pundits. He acted as if he had direct access to all the intelligence reports although he had failed to get re-elected and was not even part of the government or the opposition. He was certain that the attack was aimed at Hazaras, and the terrorists had somehow missed their target. On BBC Urdu, Dr. Abu Bakr Baloch was similarly explaining that the assailants wanted to kill Shias only and they had even ordered the Sunnis to go away from the site of the attack.

In a society where attacks on the minority Hazaras have become a routine, these statements seem to be based on the lazy presumption that the Hazaras are always the target. It seemed as if the most intriguing question was not who the terrorists were or why the security institutions had failed to prevent such an attack but rather, how the terrorists had missed their routine target the Hazara. It seems the society has normalized the massacre of the Hazaras, and that people were only curious to know how the attackers missed the Hazaras. It seemed the larger citizenry had nothing to worry about as long as the terrorists were accurate in targeting the Hazaras. Such statements from multiple corners are lazy at best and apologetic to the terrorists at worst. These comments were also in contrast to the official statement on BBC Urdu issued by the terrorists who claimed that this attack was to avenge the murder of a family in the Kharotabad incident. Lashkar-e-Jhangavi (LeJ) issued detailed statements in the dailies in which it was clearly stated that the attack on June 15 was to avenge the Kharotabad incident. These statements explained that the female students were particularly chosen as targets to avenge the deaths of Ayesha and Hafsa, a woman and a girl, who were among those killed by the Frontier Corps personnel at a check post in Kharotabad.

Deputy Commissioner of Quetta, Abdul Mansoor Kakar, also lost his life in the indiscriminate firing that happened at BMC. LeJ terrorists had positioned themselves on the roof of the complex and they showered bullets down onto the rescuers and the administration onsite. DC Kakar was among the many who lost their lives. Urdu language daily Jang published a detailed story the next day in which a friend of the martyred DC Kakar explained that Abdul Mansoor had been killed because he wanted the massacre of Hazaras to stop. The editor of the paper must have found this piece of the revelation super interesting therefore he published it as an eye-catching headline. People are confused about whom to believe. The LeJ terrorists who claim to have perpetrated this as revenge for the murder of the mujahid family in Kharotabad or senator Hasil Bizenjo and Dr. Abu Bakar Baloch who claim this incident was solely about the Hazaras.

There is no denying the fact that if the diagnosis is wrong, treatment cannot be accurate. The Hazara community has been at the receiving end of genocidal violence for almost thirteen years now. Each of us can explain multiple hypotheses and be simultaneously correct as well since there can be multiple factors at play. From international powers to local mafias, multiple actors can be involved in this genocide and so competing narratives exist. But one thing remains certain: despite the hundreds of deaths, the Hazaras have maintained their resolve to protest injustice and terrorism with non-violence. We have maintained utmost discipline and never resorted to violence. I hope I am not wrong in my expectation that our fellow citizens should not single out the Hazaras as the focal point of analysis for every act of terrorism. Victim blaming, sweeping facts away, dissociating yourselves for the fear of being killed, and leaving out the Hazaras on their own to deal with terrorism is nothing but a failed attempt to bury your heads in the sand.

Our neighbours have to realize that a fire in the neighbourhood will eventually burn down their nests too. People who insist that the terrorists intended to target the Hazaras and, only by an accident, they hit the wrong bus, are promoting a delusion that terrorism will not affect them. The terrorists themselves are clear in their assertion that they had acted with unmistakable planning and acted in full accordance with their plan. In the face of a clear statement from the perpetrators, statements from Hasil Bizenjo and others seem to dishonestly pacify the majority citizenry that they should not worry much about the ongoing wave of terrorism since they are not the ultimate targets. These apologetic explanations are morally corrupt and factually inaccurate.

It is high time citizens of Pakistan in general, and residents of Balochistan and Quetta, in particular, realized that our enemies are common. Our divisions only benefit our enemies. If we did not step in to extend solidarity to each other and raise a voice against terrorism, no one will be spared. Martin Luther King Jr. once said, "We must learn to live together as brothers or perish together as fools".

Main aaj zad pe agar hoon tou khush-gumaan na ho
Cheragh sab kay bujhengay, hawa kisi ki naheen
(Come out of delusion for if I am on target today...
The storm is a friend to none, it will ultimately extinguish everybody's lantern)

June 16, 2013

II

Shootout at BMC

On a fateful Saturday in June, Quetta city was drenched in red once again. The stench of blood and gunpowder filled the air one more time. And with that, the ephemeral tranquillity of the city gave way to the omnipotent fear. As I watched with agony the television footage of remains of one Sardar Bahadur Khan Women University's bus and its innocent students wrapped in a white shroud, I was gripped by the sense of déjà vu. It felt as if the scenes of the horrendous attack on a bus of the Balochistan University of Information Technology and Engineering Management Sciences (BUITEMS) in June 2012, and one pilgrimage bus in December the same year, had been replayed. The charred bodies, amputated limbs scattered around, and the whines of the injured; everything looked so similar. As I was clustering my thoughts, the news of a second bomb blast pulled my attention back to the television screen. This time the target was BMC's emergency ward, where the victims of the earlier bombing had been brought for treatment. The suicide attack had claimed many innocent lives including those of DC Quetta, a doctor, and three paramedics.

The modus operandi of the attacks seemed eerily similar to the one in April of 2010, outside the emergency ward of civil hospital. Syed Nasir Shah, the then MNA from our locality, had narrowly escaped but the suicide attack had killed a news channel cameraman, four police personnel, and over a dozen of innocent civilians. Earlier the same day, a banker had been targeted on Qandahari Bazar. The plot was similar; the first attack, it seemed, was a ploy to get the actual targets to the desired location, and the second attack to terminate them.

My train of thoughts was soon interrupted by the chaos-stricken crowd rushing on my TV screen. Some perpetrators had taken a position on the hospital roof, wherefrom, they were spraying bullets and grenades on the civilians inside the hospital premises. Surprisingly, this mode of attack wasn't novel either. We had borne witness to an incident in March 2004, when the annual congregation of Ashura was hit similarly. Assailants, positioned on top of the buildings on both sides of the Liaquat Bazar, had initially attacked the mourners with heavy artillery, and later had jumped off the roof exploding their suicide waists meanwhile That incident claimed more than 40 lives with over 100 causalities. In another attack in September of 2010, at Mizan Chowk, a suicide bomber had blown himself in Quds rally, causing massive panic in the crowd, only to be followed by an excessive spray of bullets by unknown assailants hiding nearby. The incident claimed more than 80 lives, while over a hundred people had been injured.[1] The cameraman of a news channel was also killed in the incident.

Back on the TV screen, I could see multiple dead bodies all clad in the white shrouds. Their faces had been covered, mutilated beyond recognition by the guns of the assailants. Nothing felt new, neither the incident nor the bullet riddled bodies of the victims. So many times, on so many occasions, the victims had been mutilated to the extent that their loved ones had failed to recognize them.

The TV screen showed a wailing old lady, crying profusely. She might have been a mother to one of the deceased. Strangely, neither her whines nor the tears rolling down her wrinkled cheeks felt unseen before. To me, she felt like those hundreds of mothers who would beat their chests in anguish for the loss of their sons to one or another terrorist incident. She was crying her eyes out the same way others did, when their sole bread-earning sons were dragged off the bus, shot at point blank and killed in cold blood in Mastung,[2] some 30 kilometers away from Quetta. Her ear-piercing shriek felt no different from the ones mourning the death of their sons, who were killed

[1] CNN Wire Staff, "Death toll from Pakistan suicide bombing rises to 73", CNN, September 4, 2010,
https://edition.cnn.com/2010/WORLD/asiapcf/09/03/pakistan.violence/.

[2] Shezad Baloch, "Sectarian atrocity: 29 killed in Mastung, Quetta ambushes", Express Tribune, September 20, 2011,
https://tribune.com.pk/story/256419/gunmen-attack-bus-in-balochistan-20-killed.

while offering prayers in mosques,[3] when commuting to home towards Hazara Town[4] or targeted by the suicide bomber who had blown a snooker club on Alamdar Road.[5] Her wails felt equally painful to the ones crying over the remains of blown-up bodies of their young. The old lady was no different from mourning mothers in the other parts of the country. She had cried inconsolably when the entire colony of the Badami Bagh in Lahore was set ablaze,[6] in a matter of hours everything from books to toys, food to furniture, humans to houses were turned to ashes. She had banged her head against the wall, when dozens of innocents were killed in an explosion in Abbas Town, Karachi.[7] I had seen her sob so many times in KPK, where children had been targeted in a series of bomb blasts.[8] I had seen her mourn the death of her son killed in buses in Chillas, Gilgit-Baltistan. With mournful

[3]David Rohde, "47 Pakistanis Die in Attack On Shiite Rites", New York Times, July 5, 2003, https://www.nytimes.com/2003/07/05/world/47-pakistanis-die-in-attack-on-shiite-rites.html.
Mohammad Zafar, "Two Hazara community members gunned down in Quetta", Express Tribune, June 04, 2017,
https://tribune.com.pk/story/1427282/two-hazara-community-members-gunned-quetta.

[4]BBC, "Pakistan blasts: Scores killed at Quetta snooker hall", BBC News, January 10, 2013, https://www.bbc.com/news/world-asia-20969443.

[5]Muhammad Faisal Ali, "125 Christian houses burnt over blasphemy", DAWN, March 09, 2013, https://www.dawn.com/news/791491/125-christian-houses-burnt-over-blasphemy.\

[6]Staff Reporter, "Blast ravages Shia neighbourhood", DAWN, March 03, 2013, https://www.dawn.com/news/790071/blast-ravages-shia-neighbourhood.

[7]Zahir Shah Sherazi, Mateen Haider, Hassan Jahangiri, Abdul Hakim, "Militant siege of Peshawar school ends, 141 killed", DAWN, December 16, 2014,
https://www.dawn.com/news/1151203.

eyes, I had seen her look up the skies and beg for mercy, when her son was killed in Data Darbar bombing in Lahore. She had wailed when her son had been shot going to his school, college or office. She was found mourning with the remains of the mutilated body of her kidnapped son.

I glared onto her face to look at her complexion closely. I leaned in to figure out where she belonged and what language she spoke? I was eager to determine her faith and find out her sect. How does she offer her prayers, does she do it arms open or folded, I yearned to determine? Sadly, I could see nothing except for the freckles and wrinkles on her poor complexion. Despite all my efforts I could only conclude that she was a mother. A mother who had been incessantly mourning, wailing and crying for years, and today she did no different.

June 19, 2013

This piece was written after students were attacked at Sardar Bahadur Khan Women University. [a]

---

[a]Uzair Khan, "Passengers hauled off buses and gunned down: 16 killed in Kohistan sectarian attack", DAWN, February 29, 2012, https://www.dawn.com/news/699097/passengers-hauled-off-buses-and-gunned-down-16-killed-in-kohistan-sectarian-attack.

12

Hazara Town bloodied yet again

Sunday, June 30, 8:00 PM

Residents of Hazara Town are enjoying the breezy evening of Quetta city after going through a very tough day under the scorching heat of the sun. Men are out for a stroll while women are busy shopping for necessities, and they are haggling with the shop owners to get the best bargain. Children in the meantime are holding their mothers' hands and they are pushing them to buy their favourite meals for tomorrow's lunch at school. In the nearby mosque, the evening prayer is about to end where hundreds of *kafirs*[1] are facing *Ka'aba*[2] in the state of prostrating to Allah. Meanwhile, a clean dressed Muslim with a whiff of *halal*[3] cologne, wearing a

---

[1] A derogatory term commonly used for non-Muslim and increasingly by the hardliner Sunni Muslims for Shias which literally means "infidel"

[2] The House of Allah in Mecca, the holiest place for Muslims of all denominations

[3] Arabic word, which means "the allowed, the permissible" in Islam

magical *Sulemani Topi,*[4] passes through the check post guarded by *farishthay*[5] without being detected. The *noorani*[6] face heads towards the Hazara Town, where Hazara *kafirs* dwell in. He gets closer to the mosque. His intention is clear to send all Hazara Shias to hell. His heart is beating anxiously. He seems fully prepared to go to heaven at the earliest possible time with his thoughts of 72 *Hurs*[7] "virgins" of paradise who have opened their arms to warmly welcome him with garlands in their hands to adorn his neck.

Thinking of erotic heaven in his mind, he chants out loudly *Allah-o Akbar* -God is great- and detonates his suicide vest which further on leaves dozens of holes in the bodies of the *kafir* mothers who are busy shopping with their *kafir* children.[8] All that remains of the children in their mothers' hands are their little fingers. Shattered bodies of the men strolling earlier can be seen laying across the blast scene. The *kafirs* who are praying in the mosque rush outside where they find nothing but the dead bodies lying across and walls painted with red blood. Soon after the blast, the government and the security establishment officials rush to the blast scene to count the "hell-bound" dead bodies and to assess the success of the attack by their

---

[4]A mythical cap which renders the one wearing the cap invisible

[5]A political hint for Pakistan Army or the military establishment

[6]From a personal name based on Arabic roots, nūrānī 'luminous', 'bright', a derivative of Arabic nūr 'light'

[7]Virgins of paradise

[8]Gul Yousufzai, "Blast in Pakistani city of Quetta kills at least 28", Reuters, July 1, 2013, https://www.reuters.com/article/us-pakistan-blast-quetta-idUSBRE95T0BT20130701.

own *Jihadi* angel "holy warrior".

The people of Hazara town on the other hand also hasten to the blast scene and start taking the dead and the injured to Bolan Medical College (BMC) hospital where they find locks on the doors of the doctors and paramedics. The dead bodies are left lying on the hospital floor while the distraught loved ones start running in the hospital to find any doctor or medical staff but all in vain. Afterward, the dead and injured are taken to other hospitals around seven kilometres away from the blast scene.

Home Secretary, later on, issues an official statement claiming the Security Staff failed to stop the *noorani* faced Muslim man who was wearing a *Burqa*.[9] It's worth mentioning that females in Hazara town do not wear *Burqa* and the Home Secretary knows it well, but it remains unknown why he claimed so. Hazara women instead wear a sarong type wrap known as *"chadar namaz"* which is way different from *Burqa*. It, therefore, defies reason to suggest that a burqa-clad man could have passed through many check-posts as a woman unless somehow, he flew past them using his angel-wings. Contradicting the Home Secretary's statement, the honourable Quetta City Police Chief (CCPO), Mir Zubair suggests that the assailant was an ethnic Uzbek who have similar Asiatic features like Hazaras.[10] According to CCPO, an Uzbek was on a

---

[9] A loose garment covering the entire body and having a veiled opening for the eyes, worn by conservative Muslim women

[10] Riaz Ahmad, Mohammad Zafar, "Vicious cycle of violence: Militants strike in Quetta, Peshawar", Express Tribune, June 30, 2013,
https://tribune.com.pk/story/570738/vicious-cycle-of-violence-militants-strike-in-quetta-peshawar

bicycle pedaling in search of heaven. The purpose of CCPO's statement is to hide the obvious by creating a "reasonable doubt" that our Muslim-attacker only succeeded in getting to the Hazaras because of similar features. However, pictures shared on Facebook showing the severed head of the *Jihadi* Muslim clearly shows he is either from Balochistan or from the "sacred-land" of South Punjab.

Visible from the picture, the trickling blood out of the severed-head of the so-called "martyr" suicide bomber lay with one eye closed as if he was trying to wink at the heavenly-virgins while the other open eye gives a mixed impression of surprise and distraught which is usually seen when someone makes a stop at a wrong station.

Monday, July 1, 2:00 PM

A stage is set in Hazara town. A large number of people, including women and children have gathered. They are watching the action-replay of the event that has been going on for years. They have seen this time and again but are forced to see it yet again. Political leaders are preparing their speeches while women are mourning and crying as if somehow, they could hold on to their loved ones from going 6-feet under. Spirited religious slogans can also be heard loudly showing their desire to achieve martyrdom. People are waiting for their leaders. They are 100% sure that once again there will be an announcement of a sit-in protest like they had after the January 10 and February 16 attacks this year. Many are hoping that once again demands handing Quetta over to the army and targeted operation against Lashkar-e Jhangvi (LeJ) will be raised.

Hazaras are also expecting religious leaders from Punjab to come forward and make fiery speeches as they did after the January 10 and February 16 attacks and will force the government to implement Governor's rule in Balochistan.

The so-called religious leaders came up with their stereo-typed speeches urging people to get united, lecturing on the worth of achieving martyrdom and their high places in heaven, declaring that the suicide bomber is destined for hell, praying to Allah to grant patience to victims' loved ones giving examples of the martyrdom of baby Ali Asghar (AS) and young Ali Akbar (AS). Those speaking of their desire for martyrdom were later found standing protected among the armed guards. Soon, many realize that there are no more situations like before. It is the first of July 2013, and it has been over one month since the elections are passed. Those who previously demanded to hand over Quetta to the Pakistan Army are themselves part of the new provincial government and expecting some kind of ministerial position in the provincial cabinet. Therefore, they cannot afford to make inconvenient demands or prolong the protest debate. In any case, the deaths of some poor and backward Hazaras could not really be that important for which their future interests could be jeopardized. Therefore, after the mandatory prayer for the deceased, the body of each *kafir* is brought in the coffin draped with shawls laced with Quranic verses and quietly laid to rest.

Like always, the banned sectarian outfit LeJ gleefully accepts responsibility for the attack and reaffirms its resolve to continue attacks till the establishment of the Islamic caliphate is accomplished in the Islamic Republic of Pakistan. From their statements, one feels that Hazaras are the only hurdle standing in the way of their "sacred mission" and, therefore, by finishing them, they are securing their rightful place in heaven.

On the other hand, people are dumbfounded on why the government has miserably failed to restore order even when there are checkpoints along every step of the way all over the city? Citizens have been demanding for a while that instead of "putting people behind the walls" and erecting checkpoints every kilometre of the way, why not go after terrorists' safe heavens? And why not make an honest effort at capturing the terrorists and bringing them to justice? Such efforts would surely bring positive results in the fight against terrorism in a small manageable city such as Quetta where strong ethnic affiliations make it a challenging environment for terrorism to take root. But people are also mindful that government and security agencies would have dismantled the terrorist network if they wanted to since they know every single one of their safe heavens is.

There is a need for the Chief Minister of Balochistan, Dr. Abdul Malik Baloch, to come up with a clear policy towards terrorism in order to stop the ongoing genocide of Hazaras happening in the guise of sectarianism; to tell the public the real intentions of the terrorists and reveal identities of those behind the terrorist outfits; to speak with the nation-states that are posing as Pakistan's friendsSaudi Arabia, United Arab Emirates, Qatar, Iranand warn them against conducting their proxy wars in Balochistan and using the Hazara nation as the fuel for their proxy war. Just like all citizens of Balochistan, the Hazaras expect Dr. Malik to raise the issue of peace in Balochistan on every forum possible. And the citizens rightfully expect that Dr. Malik will not let them down.

This article was originally published on Hazara.Net

This is a translation of an Urdu article by Hasan Riza Changezi regarding the AL Qaeda affiliated 'Lashkar-e Jhangvi terrorist attack targeting Hazara Town on June 30, 2013.

The original Urdu version of the article captures the before and after scenes of the terrorist attack from a Hazara point of view. An edited version of the article in Urdu was published by the Dawn News.[11] When quoting the author, please only refer to the original article in Urdu.

13

The Ultimate Salvation

In my childhood, there was only one television channel, the Pakistan TV abbreviated as PTV. As the only channel available, we would watch every single program from *Baseerat*[1] to *Farman-e-Elahi*.[2] Occasionally, PTV would broadcast a classical music program by the name of Rag Rang sometime around midnight. Lack of an alternative channel would tempt us to watch the program even when we had zero taste in the genre of classical music. My mother wasn't quite fond of the program either. So, whenever the program was aired on the television, she would instantly leave the room, all the while mumbling something that only she could decipher. Curious as I was, when I asked her opinion about the program one day, she unleashed a torrent of curses upon the singers. She thought they were too old to be of indulging in such profanities. She especially abhorred the way the old

[1] recitation of Quranic verses to start the transmission

[2] recitation of Quranic verses to end the daily transmission

lads contorted their faces to sing, the sound of which to her was cacophony.

My mother's voice still echoes in my head, especially when I am scanning the television channels and see an eager researcher exploring the Amazon biome, studying the endangered species of crocodiles; or when I find a passionate woman walking barefoot on the muddy paths in a remote jungle in search of an anaconda. My mother's words strike my mind over and over again, particularly when I am watching a program about a passionate sea diver exploring the underwater world or carrying out studies on the collective behaviour of fish. Or when I see some zealous zoologists tramping up and down the mountains, deserts, caves, and forests in search of bats, ants, lizards, snakes, birds, and insects. At times, I am astonished to see them waste their time in such petty indulgences instead of serving the will of God.

My mother's words linger in my head when I get to watch a documentary about Stephen Hawking. The man cannot even wipe the drool that drips off his mouth. Diagnosed with motor neuron disease at an early age, he is assisted by a nurse for his basic daily activities like eating, drinking, taking care of personal hygiene, and getting dressed. Instead of using his time remembering the Almighty, he wastes it in unveiling the secrets of the universe. Owing to his disability, he needs to spend more time praying and beseeching God for his good health and forgiveness of his sins. In fact, better he should consult a *Mawlawi*[3] who could lead

---

[3]Muslim religious scholar

him to a divine guidance; help him seek salvation in the hereafter and enlighten him on the complexities of the mighty universe; albeit in a plain language.

I say this with utmost conviction because I myself used to go to a local *madrassa* with my fellows, during our school holidays. One day when we were all busy memorizing our lessons, we felt a tremor. All panicked, we wanted to flee but the *Mawlawi* scolded and then forbade us from leaving the room. Later that day, when asked by one of my classmates about the cause of the earlier jolt, *Malawi saheb* explained how this mother earth is balanced on the horns of some buffalo that itself is standing on the back of a fish that is swimming in the ocean. When the buffalo attempts to shift the world from one horn to the other, it triggers an earthquake. The Malawi then added that the jolts are also a punishment from Almighty for the sins of humanity. The righteous and the virtuous would receive no harm, while there is no escape from God's wrath for the sinners. It is thus pointless to run for your life when the earthquake strikes. At the end of the day's lesson when we were leaving for home, a quirky kid whispered to the others that *Mawlawi* probably forbade us to escape because he himself is impaired. He would have been the first one to run for his life if he had not been paralyzed.

On another occasion, replying to a question about thunder and lightning, the *Mawlawi* explained that when Allah commands the rain angel to shower some rain, the angel kicks the sky, and thus lightning strikes. The sky then roars and cries in pain which results in the form of rain. Fast forward to our time in the university where we had subjects like geology and geography as part of our curriculum, which enlightened us with scientific explanations on the causes of natural disasters such as storms and earthquakes. Safe to say *Mawlawi Saheb's* explanations were much easier to comprehend and thus are still afresh in my memory, compared to the hefty scientific details that I learned at the university which have now totally escaped my memory.

It is strongly suggested to Stephen Hawking and his ilk to stop wasting their time studying and researching about the complexities of the universe, theoretical physics, black holes, fourth dimension, time travel, and black particle or more accurately God particle; and instead, start making good use of their time pondering about the life in the hereafter. As far as exploration of the universe is concerned, I suggest them to consult a *Mawlawi* who could enlighten them on the phenomenon in such simple and plain language that they would never forget.

I strongly recommend the zoologists conducting research on insects, birds, snakes, and crocodiles to stop their aimless activities at once and spend the rest of their lives praying to Allah, repenting, and then seeking forgiveness for their sinful practices. In their noble pursuit of salvation, they may join a *Tableeghi Jamaat*,[4] or may certainly choose to live in Pakistan, the land of purity. This country is the fortress of Islam; welcomes those who seek to do good and leads them to

---

[4]Islamic missionary movement

84

paradise. I am sure, after living in this dear homeland for a while, seeing the unpredictability, humiliation, and misery of life, they will lose faith in humanity. Consequently, they will not only leave their futile indulgence but also, might switch their interest from exploring the universe and attempting to save the endangered species of animals, to follow the right path that could ultimately lead them to heaven.

This is a piece of satire and was first published on DAWN Urdu website on August 28, 2013.[5]

[5]Hasan Riza Changezi, "بھینسے کا سینگ...فرشتے کی لاٹ", DAWN Urdu, August 28, 2013,

Http://www.dawnnews.tv/news/119257/bhainse-ka-seeng-farishte-ki-laat-riza-changezi-aq.

14

All Talk and No Action!

I am known as a braggart and a half-wit to my friends. They all seem to have reached a consensus that when it comes to boasting, I'm unrivalled. Hence, whenever I give my two cents on some serious issue, all my friends start nudging each other and the debate turns into a petty argument. Everyone tends to change the topic; one brings up the issue of inflation by discussing the rising food prices while another changes the notion to talk about Aamir Liaquat Hussain (Pakistani TV host and Former Minister of Religious Affairs of Pakistan). Only a couple of days ago, in a heated debate at a friend's place, all of us agreed that we should thank no one but Allah for running the Islamic Republic of Pakistan. The deteriorating law and order coupled with the dismal state of governance go a great deal to prove that the sole nuclear power in the Muslim world and the so-called 'Fortress of Islam' is on the verge of collapse. Each of my friends had his reasons to believe; so, to back up their statements, one of them reffered to Dera Ismail Khan Prison break.[1] Another pointed to tragic incidents of Quetta while the other highlighted the lawlessness that runs through the width and breadth of this country, from Khyber to Karachi.

Referring to the newly elected government, a friend mentioned Prime Minister Nawaz Sharif's maiden visit to Quetta. During his visit, the Prime Minister had argued that Quetta was a small city consisting only of few markets and fewer lanes and, therefore, be deemed as a test case to wipe out the terrorists through coordinated efforts.[2] Soon after he left, the terrorists wreaked havoc on the lives of the innocent citizens. As per one of my friends, the Prime Minister's statement had been taken more seriously by the terrorists than their law enforcer counterparts. Our debate took an emotional turn when one of my friends delivered a long and fiery speech on the theatrics staged by one-armed man, Sikandar, in the capital city of Islamabad some days ago.[3] His speech touched some nerves and almost had me lose my faith. As a true patriot, I felt responsible to help them restore their faith in the country. Even though I was quite sure

[1] BBC News, "Pakistan jailbreak: Taliban free 248 in Dera Ismail Khan", BBC News, July 30, 2013,
https://www.bbc.co.uk/news/world-asia-23493323.

[2] The Express TRIBUNE, "Balochistan crises: Nawaz directs ISI, IB to catch Hazara Town bombers", The Express TRIBUNE, July 02, 2013,
https://tribune.com.pk/story/571395/hazara-tragedy-nawaz-sharif-visits-quetta-to-discuss-security-situation.

[3] The Guardian, "Pakistani politician cheered and jeered for leaping on gunman", The Guardian, August 16, 2013,
Https://www.theguardian.com/world/2013/aug/16/pakistani-politician-leaped-on-gunman

of being taken lightly, I intended to try. Sure- enough that they won't believe a single word I say, I, nonetheless, kept trying to convince them. To demonstrate my point, I reminded them of how after taking control of Swat, Taliban had imposed harsh Islamic rules in the name of Sharia Law in the region providing people with swift justice at their doorsteps. Instead of the Pakistani flag, the Taliban's flag was hoisted over police stations and other government buildings. In an attempt to align the traffic laws in accord to Islamic principles, growing beard was deemed obligatory for traffic wardens. Hair salons were directed to trim beards and cut hair in accordance with the Islamic Sharia Law. Women were not allowed to step outside, and if they did, they were flogged in public. Music and CD shops were bombed along with their owners. In the Islamic state, beheading the opponents became a regular occurrence. Many were left with hopelessness and sheer despair. They believed that the writ of the state was no longer existent and if the country was still running, it was run by no one but Allah.

In the recent past, when rumours were rife that the Taliban militants were fast approaching the Margalla Hills,[4,5] our enemies claimed that if that happened it would then be a matter of time before they

[4]The News, "Matters of war, life and death", The News, August 31, 2009, https://www.thenews.com.pk/archive/print/194133-matters-of-war-life-and-death.

[5]Aryn Baker, "Taliban Advance, Is Pakistan Nearing Collapse", TIME, April 23, 2009, Http://content.time.com/time/world/article/0,8599,1893370,00.html.

got control of the country's nuclear arsenal. The safety of the nuclear weapon seemed more concerning than anything else to them. Fortunately, the government and state officials realised it was about time they applied the iron fist policy and bring the terrorists on the right path. Consequently, they launched an operation to banish the Taliban from Swat valley and took back its control.[6] I personally believe if the government and state agencies have the will power, they have the capability to rid the country of the menace of terrorism. If Pakistan can counter India, a country with military size twice that of Pakistan's and comprising an area four times bigger than Pakistan, then exterminating a few thousand terrorists must not be difficult for the atomic power. If they can spot and kill senior and prominent Baloch leader Nawab Akbar Bugti in his secluded hideout,[7] then it must not be hard for them to start a crackdown on well-known terrorists and teach them a lesson. Despite having prior information, if the authorities failed to prevent DI Khan prison break or if they didn't pay heed to the terrorists' threats in Quetta, which claimed the lives of over forty policeman including high ranking officers, then I have a strong faith in the notion that these events

---

[6]Tim Craig, "The Taliban once ruled Pakistan's Swat Valley. Now peace has returned", The Washington Post, May 09, 2015,
https://www.washingtonpost.com/world/the-taliban-once-ruled-pakistans-swat-valley-now-peace-has-returned/2015/05/08/6bb8ac96-eeaa-11e4-8050-839e9234b303_story.html

[7]Saleem Shahid, "Bugti killed in operation: Six officers among 21 security personnel dead", DAWN News, August 27, 2006,
https://www.dawn.com/news/207726/bugti-killed-in-operation-six-officers-among-21-security-personnel-dead.

must have been allowed to happen to secure our national interest. Otherwise, if the incidents had not been prevented, it must have been God's will.

Obviously, it was not a child's play to free more than one hundred hard-core militants from Dera Ismail Khan Prison[8] and transfer them into a safer place. The criminals who were previously on the death row; turning them into suicide bombers would not be hard either. Associating these incidents with intelligence failure or alluding to state agencies being accomplices to the crimes is nothing but a complete misconception. We must not forget that there are many countries including India that would go to any lengths to inflict harm on Pakistan. As patriotic citizens we must have a blind faith in the government and the political parties that believe the terrorists involved in the killings could be anyone but Muslims. In-fact, Israel and other enemies of Islam that are envious of our exemplary peace and prosperity, should be blamed instead. The least we could do is so concur with the remarks by Imran Khan and Syed Munawar Hassan (Jamaat-i-Islami Chief) to justify the bombings of public and religious places as the reaction to the American drones. As per the duo, we should be grateful to the suicide bombers who have the courage to sacrifice their lives to avenge the attacks of the American drone strikes. To perform this sacred task if they kill a few thousand Pakistanis out of 180 million, we must not make a big

---

[8] Zahir Shah Sherazi, "Pakistani Taliban free over 175 inmates in DI Khan jailbreak", DAWN News, July 30, 2013,

https://www.dawn.com/news/1032777.

deal out of it. I still believe that if our state institutions have the will, they can solve the issues. We just have to wait and watch until they realize that "enough is enough."

I was articulating these arguments when I suddenly realized that all my friends were rolling their eyes and simultaneously discussing the rising food prices.

September 3, 2013

This is a piece of satire.

The original article was first published on DAWN Urdu website on September 3, 2013.

15

Let's draft a new constitution

believe it is about time this country had a new constitution. Not because the foster children of this land - the sons of the lesser Gods - mainly the Baloch, are left alienated with the existing one, but because the real sons of the land, namely the Taliban, deem it un-Islamic and non-sharia compliant. Maybe this is why they are reluctant to a dialogue with the government.[1] Despite the latter's persistence, it seems that the ever pampered and cosseted boys have gone rogue. They cannot be lured in by toys or other knick-knacks, it seems. One wonders then, maybe that is why they keep orchestrating deadly attacks time and again and blow-up places all across to express their anger. The government's top and frankly the only priority, however, has been the initiation of the

---

[1]Zahir Shah Sherazi, "Pakistani Taliban reject peace talks with govt", DAWN, November 26, 2012,
https://www.dawn.com/news/766841/ttp-reject-peace-talks.

dialogues. We as the populace are keeping our fingers crossed for the successful end to this endeavour by the government, so there may be peace in and around the country.

Given that years of love and supreme fondness have only spoiled the blue-eyed boys, we cannot, however, be stern to them as they have been groomed with great care and hard work. If they do not accept the existing constitution, we have to find alternate ways to appease our beloved assets. In this noble pursuit, it would be appropriate that we cater to their complaints and for the ultimate success of our moot, formulate a new constitution for them. Even better if we entrusted them with the responsibility of preparing a new constitution altogether. This way they would not object to any of its parts and would have no excuse to shun our offer to dialogue.

Even though we are all quite sure that our Taliban brethren have had their venerated and holy version of the constitution readied long ago - foreseeing the times like these - we still hope that our government can include the following suggestions to their list while drafting the new constitution. This would serve as a good confidence-building measure and who knows, might as well pave the way for success in the subsequent dialogues.

1-   As is known, our Taliban brethren want to rename this country as Emarat Islami Pakistan (Islamic Emirate of Pakistan). Far better it would be, if they named it Doulat Al-Emarat Al-Bakistania Al Mutahida Al-Islamia, for it fits well with the injunctions of the Sharia and is also brimmed with such holiness that with a single articulation a man can rid himself off of all his past sins. .

2- Like the city of Islamabad, containing the words Islam, or Faisalabad, named after the diseased guardian of the Holy Mosque, King Faisal of Saudi Arabia; the rest of the cities across the country should have their unholy names redone to Islamic format.

3- The existing names of the four provinces are a constant source of regional discord and breed racial prejudices which is totally against the Islamic teachings. They should be re-named after some pious personnel from the annals of Islam.

4- Islam doesn't accept any frontiers so the borders of the new Emirate should be open to all the Muslims across the globe, especially to the holy crusaders. With this, to maintain its purity, non-Muslims should be barred from entry.

5- The use of all scientific inventions including electricity, on account of them being un-Islamic and Sharia non-compliant, should be banned. Instead, people should be encouraged to live their lives in simplicity as advised by Sharia. It is imperative thus that the new constitution should ban the use of not just cars, bicycles, and motorcycles but airplanes and locomotives too. Instead, the use of camels, horses, and donkeys should be appreciated for the purpose of transportation.

6- Since Jews and other heretics have long been conspiring to formulate a medicine that could physically harm and make the righteous Muslims impotent, the new constitution should prohibit the use of medicines and any medical types of equipment altogether. Anybody violating this should be penalized by flagellation in public.

7- For the spiritual welfare and soul healing of the masses, Islamic treatments should be promoted. People associated with such businesses should be awarded special concessions and grants so that the masses could benefit from their services.

8- Because many of the diseases are caused by the wrongdoings of evil jinns and witches; spiritual healers are thus of utmost importance. It is better to have dedicated organizations, spread across the Emirate, where aspirants of witchcraft and voodoos could be schooled and trained in the art.

9- The new constitution should oblige all men to wear a prayer cap, a kufi cap, or some headgear and have their trousers folded up above their ankles. All other dresses which are sharia non-compliant ought to be banned and anyone violating it should be flogged in public.

10- Men's beard, women's purdah and our pious Taliban brethren's perspective about the apostates are crystal clear. These subjects are beyond any discussion, and nobody needs to opine on them. Women, however, can be trained in the art of making improvised explosive devices (IEDs) and suicide vests. This can serve them with the means of acquiring a livelihood for themselves and their families.

11- All the places of worship of the non-believers are blown up and demolished by locally made IEDs. Mosques should then be built in their places instead. Likewise, schools should be replaced by madrassas across the country.

12- Most of the sports are pioneered by non-Muslims. Therefore, most do not abide by the Islamic code of dressing. Thus, all sports must be banned in the Emirate. Instead, archery, wrestling, and spearing should be promoted only if the participants adhere to the Islamic way of dressing.

13- Camel race is a popular sport in most of the Arab world. It should be raised to the status of the national sports of the Emirate, hence. To seal a pardon in the world hereafter, since they could fall off and run over by the mighty camels, the jockeys better be a non-Muslim toddler.

14- Per the new constitution, all newspapers should be banned. Every man in the Emirate should instead have a Halal radio fitted with a Halal battery, both being made in an Islamic land by our Muslim brethren. Moreover, the said radio should only play halal FM. This would help keep the populace updated with the latest fatwas. Telephone and wireless devices should be strictly banned, instead, pigeons should be trained and used for the purpose of communication.

15- Friday should be our off day. As an entertainment

for the masses, each Friday after the obligatory mass prayers, a congregation of some sort in which the non-believers could be flogged and the defectors are beheaded, could be arranged.

16- On the holy occasion of Eid-ul-Azha, the slaughtering of the non-believers should be made permissible alongside the usual sacrifice of animals. This would ensure that those who couldn't afford to purchase animals otherwise, can still fulfil their religious obligation by slaughtering an apostate.

For the formulation of the constitution and the success of the dialogue, it would be wise of the government to seek the help of Imran Khan and Munawar Hassan. The said duo have a knack for defending the Taliban and preach their message in expressions far better than the Taliban themselves. Together they make an excellent choice for advisors or spokesmen for the Taliban polity in the future.

The proverbial ball is in the government's court since the Taliban have brazenly refused to accept the current constitution of Pakistan. Given that the former does provide a sharia-compliant constitution at the whims of the latter, we can certainly cherish peace in our country, one that could parallel the harmony of a graveyard.

Note: This is a piece of satire. Despite, or because of, all the devastation and bombing of civilians and law enforcement agencies, the government had been apologetic and had been pressing for negotiations with the Taliban. The latter, however, were persistent in their refusal to negotiate with the government under the current constitution.

The original article was first published on DAWN Urdu website on October 22, 2013.[2]

---

[2]Hasan Riza Changezi, " آئیں ایک نیا آئین بنائیں ", DAWN Urdu, October 22, 2013,

Https://www.dawnnews.tv/news/130854/lets-draft-a-new-constitition-for-pakistan-riza-changezi-aq.

16

We are a dead nation

God has blessed us with many good qualities. One of our exceptional qualities is that we don't possess any bad quality. Even if we do, we don't acknowledge them. Therefore, we have a hard time to rectify our mistakes, because we never own them. Consequently, we keep on repeating the same mistakes. We are unparalled when it comes to blowing our own trumpet. Whether or not we have the capability for doing anything extraordinary, but we are the best at blowing ourselves out of proportion. We have blindfolded ourselves, but no one can compete with us in farsightedness. We don't even realize that as a nation we have been going around in circles, but we are in a state of self-delusion that we are leading the caravan. We have turned deaf ears to everything else except the sound of the same bell that we have tied around our necks. We are suffering from misapprehension that God has his special grace on us.

We strongly believe that we are extraordinary creatures of God who solely created us to lead the world. Therefore, we, ourselves, have put many feathers in our cap and have chosen magnificent titles for us without ever knowing what they stand for.

There are 197 sovereign states, fifty seven of these are Muslim countries. Besides western African countries, the Islamic Republic of Mauritania, the Islamic Republic of Iran, and the Islamic Republic of Afghanistan, Pakistan has the honour of being the Islamic Republic. Ironically, most of the Arab countries prefer to be known as the Arab States and Republics. I wonder why Bengalis deprived themselves of the heavenly blessings of the sole Islamic Republic of ours by divorcing us after much bloodshed. It is difficult to know why the Baloch population is not ready to appreciate the divine blessings of this holy place. This question still awaits an answer that why children, elderly, women, and daily wagers from the Hazara community are killed in this divine republic on everyday basis? Why are the Ahmadi and Christian communities not safe in Pakistan, and why have the Hindus been migrating from this country to save their daughters from sexual abuse and forced conversions by their Muslim abductors?

We take pride in labelling our country, Pakistan, the forte of Islam. I have no idea who, why, and when was it announced to be a forte of Islam where every other individual is infidel just because they have been declared so by the other sects; where people are engaged in a mad race to declare each other infidels or apostates; where in the name of Islam, opponents are decapitated mercilessly every day; where mosques, imambargahs, shrines, and even the funerals are hit by suicide bombers, who, while chanting the slogan "God is Great," blow themselves up and turn the bodies of children, elderly, and women into pieces. How can we call it a fort of Islam where places of worship of non-Muslims are not safe; where bones and the remains are taken out of the graves and sold out; where the meat of dogs, cats, and other abominable and dead animals are cooked and sold in restaurants and hotels; where teeth of dead animals are used to make human teeth and their fat is used in producing ghee; where infant milk powder is made by a mixture of fertilizers, chemicals, and hair removing creams and where life-saving drugs are made by amalgamating chalks, flours, sugar, and tap water.

I don't understand what do we want to substantiate by declaring a country as the forte of Islam which is included in the list of forty most corrupt countries in the world? A country where corrupt politicians use fake degrees to get elected to the parliament only to carry out legislation for the citizenry and where billions of rupees in pension money of the low scale employees are devoured by bureaucracy as their legitimate right. In a country where Islamic scholars do not hesitate to sell decrees under Mozariba and in the name of Islamic Banking to simplistic Muslims and devour millions of rupees; where a large number of the poor can be seen begging on every second step of the way; where hundreds and thousands of people are compelled to sleep on footpaths; where mothers are crushed during a stampede as they gather to receive charity to feed their kids; where you can't get your legitimate work done by the public servants without bribing them; where the lawmakers[1] are lawbreakers; where the watchman joins hands with the burglars to break into the houses for stealing; where the rich provide their pets with imported food, and the poor search for their daily bread in the garbage.

We are proud of the fact that our country is the only atomic power in the Islamic world. However, we forget to mention that in literacy, we stand at 113th out of 120 countries.[2] Almost 60% of the people are living below the poverty line, says a report of World Bank. Around 13% of the children under the age of five are malnourished due to lack of sufficient food. We are not able to provide enough electricity for our people. Factories are closing down due to the chronic shortages of electricity and gas. We are unable to treat dengue fever and Congo viruses which result in many deaths annually. Hundreds of people die due to the shortage of medical facilities. At the same time, our ruling elites prefer to get their treatment done from foreign countries. The child mortality rate is 25%, which is the highest in South Asia.[3] According to the World Health Organisation (WHO), half of the population does not have access to drinking water.[4] Similarly, around 22% of population does not have

---

[1] The News, "Agency men found involved in kidnapping of traders", The News, August 29, 2013, https://www.thenews.com.pk/Todays-News-13-25081-Agency-men-found-involved-in-kidnapping-of-traders.

[2] DAWN News, "Literacy and Pakistan", DAWN News, May 22, 2013,https://www.dawn.com/news/1012884/literacy-and-pakistan.

access to toilets. In the rural areas of Balochistan and Sindh, people have no choice but to share the same pond with animals to get their drinking water. The road in far-flung areas is so worn out that it takes the whole day to cover a few hours journey. The security situation is so adverse that Pakistan is listed among the most dangerous countries in the world. Many are killed in bomb blasts, suicide bombings and target killings every other day. The government's writ is non-existent in many areas of Baluchistan, Karachi,[5] and the tribal areas.

Terrorists keep challenging the writ of the state. However, the government, instead of taking any action against them, is being apologetic to them. These terrorists have no fear of Pakistan's military and civil administration. They are only terrified of the American drones, operated by a few individuals who while enjoying the leisure of their offices are busy playing video games like kids. Our government always blames the foreign countries for the deteriorating law and order situation in the country. Being an atomic power, if we cannot counter the ill intentions of our enemies, then how wise is it to spend a large sum of taxpayer's money on such atomic nuclear program? Currently, we

[3]Express News, "علاقے میں بچوں کی شرح اموات کے حوالے سے پاکستان سرفہرست ہوگیا", Express News, October 28, 2013, https://www.express.pk/story/189947/.

[4]World Health Organization, WHO Country Cooperation Strategies and Briefs https://www.who.int/country-cooperation/what-who-does/strategies-and-briefs/en/.

[5]Pak Tribune, "PM Nawaz orders agencies to abolish no-go areas in Karachi", Pak Tribune, September 04, 2013, http://old.paktribune.com/news/PM-Nawaz-orders-agencies-to-abolish-no-go-areas-in-Karachi-262798.html.

are no longer in a position to impress anyone by our nuclear program. On the contrary, we break our bones to convince the world that our nuclear power is safe enough from any terrorist infiltration.

It is one of our best qualities that we consider ourselves wise enough to be beyond criticism. If someone criticizes us, then instead of listening to him, we declare him anti-state and anti-Islam. We have a bad habit of poking our nose in other peoples' problems, but we have left our issues to others to get them fixed for us. Our politicians are not less than anyone else in this matter. They do whatever it takes to be in the public limelight. Instead of leading the people, they prefer to follow their footprints. However, they claim to be leading the caravan of people to its destination.

If we want to be a dignified nation, we need to shun hypocrisy. We ought to give ears to criticism; acknowledge our weaknesses and rectify our shortcomings otherwise we will achieve nothing from blowing our own trumpet.

The original article was published on DAWN Urdu website on November 07, 2013.[6]

[6]Hassan Riza Changezi, "ہم مردہ قوم ہیں", DAWN Urdu, November 07, 2013, Https://www.dawnnews.tv/news/134326/ham-murda-qaum-hain-riza-changezi-aq.

17

Then everything changed

People breathed a sigh of relief after the *Ashura*[1] in Quetta ended safely. But the horrific incident that happened in Rawalpindi saddened the whole country.[2] After the incident, as usual, a cycle of blame game started, and the sectarian forces tried to exploit the situation as much as they could. A storm of impudence kicked off on social media. That reminded me of 80's era. Those were the days when my friends and I were improvident and fond of hanging as our parents loved to put it. I had friends belonging to both Shia and Sunni sects and I don't remember if we had ever engaged in a sectarian discourse with each other. Life was passing as normal. Many of my Shia friends used to go to a local

[1]Ashura is the tenth day of Muharram, the first month in Islamic calendar. It is a major holy day and occasion for pilgrimage in Shia Islam.

[2]Al Jazeera, Deadly attack on Shia procession in Pakistan", Al Jazeera, November 16, 2013, Https://www.aljazeera.com/news/2013/11/16/deadly-attack-on-shia-procession-in-pakistan.

religious seminary wearing Sherwani while my Sunni friends wearing white hat used to attend lessons on Holy Quran at a local Mosque in the evenings. I don't recall if we had ever discussed such topics regarding sects. In fact, no one was ever interested to know which sect the others adhered to.

Not only we would go for picnic together but also observed Muharram rituals together. Even our Sunni friends would attend Muharram rituals regularly with us. On the other hand, children studying in a nearby madrassa would collect food items for their fellow students by knocking on every door in the neighbouring area yelling "Tukki rowdy khair usi", (giving alms would cherish you) and like every other mom, my mother would always give them something. It was not customary yet to deliver deafening sermons on loudspeakers of the mosques and imambargahs in those days. On the tenth of Moharram (the Ashura Day), the Shias would mourn, and Sunnis would take up the responsibility of arranging and distributing alms. Haji Rafiq of Chakwal Saloon and Public Showers was closed for its usual business on the Day of Ashura as it was busy warming water to provide free showers for all the mourners from dawn to dusk.

Then everything changed imperceptibly. As a repercussion of General Zia's Islamization policies of Pakistani state and Islamic revolution of Iran, the hatred in people's hearts grew deeper with the rise of louder sermons from mosques and imambargahs. As the beard grew longer in size; people's tones turned more and more unpleasant and the language instead of conveying messages of love, uttered hatred. For the very first time we were made to believe that by being born to Shia families and adhering to Shia sect make us the only virtuous creature in front of Allah and true followers of Ahl al-Bayt and our Sunni friends were made to believe that Jannah (Paradise) was exclusively for them. In those days, movement for implementing Ja'fari jurisprudence on national level was in its full swing and slogans to turn Pakistan, Quetta, in particular, into Lebanon were frequently chanted. In order to lead the show for ten days of Muharram, organisers of some imambargahs indulged in a race to hire professional preachers from Punjab and Sindh provinces at exorbitant prices. Special advertisement mentioning the amount paid to preacher was made public in order to assemble large crowds of people to give ear to the sermons. I remember one of the most expensive preachers, named Najafi who was speaking in Imambargah Hazara Kalan (Hazara Central Imambargah) got trendy in those days. He was paid forty thousand rupees currently worth 1.5 million rupees only for ten days of Muharram. He was adept at making fun of reverend personalities in a satirical way. He was second to none in blaspheming them. We, Shia friends were among his devotees. One day, a friend of mine asked him a question on a piece of paper about why do we prostrate on Mohr (a hard piece of mud form Karbala used during prayers)? The preacher narrated a story in response to his question. He stated, "Once, I was passing through a village in Punjab. At prayers time, I went to a Sunni Mosque. I laid down my prayer rug and put Mohr for prostration, I felt that the imam of the mosque was on tenterhooks and was wandering around with anxiety and anger. After I completed my prayers, he came to me and enquired about why I prostrated on this small piece of hard mud?" I replied, "Prostrating on this clay from Karbala causes anger to Satan. Did it cause you anger?" While he said this, the whole Imambargah echoed with the slogan "Naarai Haideri", needless to say, my loud voice was also included in the rallying cry. Like many others I did not comprehend at the time how the preacher evaded replying to our question cunningly. For the first time I heard cursing of the first, second and third Caliph of Islam in those days and then heard it time and again on different occasions afterwards. It was one of those days, when stones were thrown on Imambargah Hazara Kalan from the Mosque opposite. I remember a person confronted the preacher telling him, "After you are done with your job, you will go back. But the animosity created as the aftermath of your sermons would make it difficult for us to live peacefully in this place. He replied, "I have done my work; now it is up to you how you do yours!" Over the next few years, he kept making fortune from his sermons and continued poisoning young minds.

Once, another fiery speaker from Punjab was invited to the Punjabi Imambargah during Moharram. The organisers of the Imambargah campaigned to promote him even before the month of Muharram started. His first quality, as it was propagated, was him being a Deobandi and his recent conversion to Shiaism "the right path". The second reason, which contributed to his popularity, was his exorbitant fees. It was publicised that he was offered to be paid 90,000 rupees

108

which made him the most expensive amongst his counterparts during that season. I may not forget his name my entire life. His name was Mazhar Deobandi, and he was a compelling speaker. One of his sayings that received a huge popularity was, "Do ask me, and I will tell you about the faults with Sunni sect of Islam because I have been a Sunni for 45 years. I have recently embraced Shia sect." That "New Shia" earned more respect than local preachers had ever gained. One day, after doing his job honestly and leaving no stone unturned in spreading sectarian hatred, Deobandi Saheb left the rostrum and headed to his small room situated in a corner of Panjabi Imambargah; my friends and I followed him. After the formal greetings, we asked our question once again about the use of Mohr during prayers, which we had earlier asked from Najafi Saheb. At first, he tried to avoid answering our question, but when we insisted; he came up with a response which I still remember. He said, "Look son! I have just converted to Shiaism, wouldn't it be better to ask this question from some experienced preacher?" But we were still so naive to comprehend that these professional preachers who earned their bread and butter from our donations, were always ready to change sects in order to make a fortune. They were actually illiterate about the rudiments of religions and instead of answering our serious question would goof around. We had no idea that they would eventually pave the way for throwing us into a blood bath.

As time passed by, the religious extremism invigorated in the wake of implementation of Nizam-i-

Mustafa by the commander of the faithful, General Zia-ul-Haq and Iranian revolution by Imam Khomeini. As a repercussion, compassion was replaced with hatred, reason was superseded with weapons and the social interaction was reciprocated through Kalashnikovs and bombs, walls of the houses were raised and to substantiate their righteousness, a competition began in importing exceptional quality of loudspeakers from Saudi Arabia and Iran. Decrees were issued and slaughtering innocent human beings became a norm. My Sunni neighbours ceased offering alms during Moharram and the voice yelling, "Tukki rowdy khair usi" also vanished. The whole atmosphere turned gloomy. Haji Rafiq closed down his Chakwal Saloon and Public Shower and moved back to Punjab. Our clean shaved teacher in school, Master Nadeem focused all his attention on growing his beard. My childhood friend parted ways with me. News of target killings became a norm in the country and people started fleeing persecution in search of safe sanctuaries. While doing so, hundreds of people died on the snowy mountains and hundred others were drowned in the sea. Bomb blasts and target killings reached to a culmination. Children and women were slaughtered. Mothers would pray for safe return of their children before leaving them to go out. But peace went off the beaten track and never came back. Peeking through the window into the past, I envisage a peaceful society, where I could go for picnic with my boyhood friends. I am in search of a society, where no one is persecuted on the grounds of his beliefs, where people are not seen as Shia, Sunni, Hindu, Muslim or Christian but as normal human beings. I want my city, Quetta, back. I would happily renounce thousands of Riyadh, Lebanon and Tehran for my Quetta. But is there anyone who could help me get my bygone Quetta back? *Hull Min Nasir Yun Surna* (Is there anybody, who could help me?)

November 25, 2013

18

The Great Satan and the Peanuts

On the 5th of July 1977, when General Zia ul-Haq deposed the elected Prime Minister Zulfikar Ali Bhutto through a military coup d'état in Pakistan, most of the people were unaware that a cataclysmic change was about to erupt in neighbouring Afghanistan. On 17th of April 1978, only after 9 months of Zia's Martial Law in Pakistan, Sardar Daoud Khan's government was overthrown[1] and the leader of the People's Democratic Party of Afghanistan (PDPA), Nur Muhammad Taraki was appointed as the first President of the Communist regime. Just after 10 months of the communist regime, on the 27th of April 1978, the King of Iran, Reza Shah Pahlavi's government was toppled down by Khomeini who entered Tehran with his slogan of the Islamic revolution.

---

[1] Rehmatullah Afghan, Abubakar Siddique, "Afghanistan Still Facing Aftershocks of 1978 Communist Coup", gandharaerefl.org, April 27, 2020, Https://gandhara.rferl.org/a/afghanistan-still-facing-aftershocks-of-1978-communist-coup/29924804.html.

Some may proclaim that the radical political changes that happened just in one and half years were mere occurrences, but the conspiracy theorists do not seem to be ready to accept this notion. They consider it to be a part of a very well-planned strategy. They believe it was part of the game of chess that both superpowers were playing. General Zia and the Communist Regime of Afghanistan were pawns in the chessboard who were immolated painfully when the time arrived. It is interesting that Iran whose favourite slogan was "Death to America" and who considered cursing America, i.e., "The Great Satan," a gracious deed and the slogan "Neither East-Nor West" as the cornerstone of her independent foreign policy could not resist but jumped and acted as pawn in the international game in accordance with the aspiration of America. As General Zia raised the motivational slogan of "Saving Islam and stopping Red Flood" and pushed the country to safeguard American interest in the name of Jihad, similarly, Iran helped America indirectly by supporting and mobilizing its proxy groups to launch Jihad against the Soviet army. Iran's involvement in Afghan Jihad was not less than a blessing for America. Tehran, on one hand, raised the slogan "Death to America", while on the other hand helped accomplish American objectives by giving military and financial assistance to the groups doing jihad against Soviets. This is a settled fact that General Zia received millions of dollars from America for his "services" which he called as 'Peanuts.' The Arab

[2]DAWN News, "US created Taliban and abandoned Pakistan, says Hillary", DAWN News, February 01, 2016,

countries were obliged to pay this and other expenses of Jihad against the Soviet Union

Hillary Clinton, the former American Secretary of State admitted the role of America in Afghan Jihad publicly and said, "We should remember today we are fighting those who we funded twenty years ago. We did this because we were fighting the Soviets, who had invaded Afghanistan. We did not want them to establish their hegemony in central Asia, therefore, we started our work. The Reagan Administration consulted Congress where Democrats were in majority. They agreed to deal with Pakistan's military and ISI to recruit Mujahedeen from Saudi Arabia and other countries who brought with them the Wahabi brand of Islam to combat the Soviet Union. As a result, the Soviet Union was defeated, and she lost billions of dollars which consequently resulted in its disintegration. We are harvesting the seeds we had sown ourselves."[2]

What role have we played in the American Jihad against the Soviet Union at the cost of peanuts? On-Page 257-262 of his book, The Bear Trap, the living legend of Afghan Jihad Brigadier Mohammad Yousaf writes, "CIA Chief William Casey had suggested sending propaganda books to Central Asia in which Soviet atrocities to Uzbeks are incorporated. But I insisted it was more effective to send a translation of the Holy Quran in Uzbek and Russian languages. In the first consignment, the CIA arranged 10,000 copies of the Holy Quran which were sent to the areas. In 1988, we demanded the CIA for more copies of the Holy Quran which they provided. Unpredictably, circumstances were proceeding in our favour. Many fervent youths asked for weapons and sought permission to commence jihad straightaway in their areas and many concurred to join Mujahideen in Afghanistan."

On pages number 157-159, in the book, Brigadier Mohammad Yusaf elaborates further on the role of Pakistan in American Jihad, "We would send Pakistan's military personnel in the Afghan Jihad. I acclaim it with surety as I was not only recruiting them but trained them as well. I want to make it clear that they were not going for surveillance purposes but being regular military personnel, they actively participated in Afghan Jihad with Afghan brethren by giving them professional pieces of advice and would work as their advisors. They were particularly trained for sabotaging gas pipelines, attacking airports with rockets, and ambushing. Typically, our team consisted of an officer, one Junior Commissioned Officer (JCOs), and one Non-Commissioned Officer (NCOs). One of them needed to have a thorough command of the Pashto language. I insisted upon every member of the team not to be apprehended. During training, our team members would wear a beard and their clothes to conceal their identity."

To make the holy Jihad a triumph, America allied with other Arab countries and formed an alliance of seven groups of Jihadists. Similarly, Iran helped to form an alliance of eight groups on the ground. These groups ruined Kabul and turned Afghanistan into a graveyard in jihad and internecine wars. People have always bewildered why Iran, the apparent arch enemy of

America, jumped in this war on her expenses to safeguard the American interests?

The idea of defeating the Soviet Union was so enchanting and pleasant to hear that Pakistan and Iran did not realize that they had put the lives of their people in many difficulties by playing the role of the mercenary army in defeating a superpower. In this chessboard, after checkmating "Polar Bear" the USSR, by giving some sacrifices of pawns and other important pieces, America left the region in a quagmire. As a result, the equilibrium of world order transformed with America being the only superpower that is head over heels like a wild bull and tramples everything underfoot wherever it goes. Except throwing the whole region into Arab and non- Arab sectarian conflicts, what else did Pakistan and Iran achieve from jumping into American war? Iran rich in oil survived American sanctions but we could not remain immune to the conflict in the name of Jihad, and it was our stupidity that rendered the whole country into a nursery of Jihad.

In pursuit of making Afghanistan our fifth province and dominating the South Asian region, we have been doing failed experiments one after another. To establish a government of our wishes, we arranged the grand finale of Mujahidin in Islamabad and sometimes we exhibited assemblies of Jihadi leaders in Peshawar. Sometimes, we made them take an oath on the holy Quran, and at another, we took an oath of their loyalty in Kaaba.[3] But when these mujahideen were

---

[3]Https://en.wikipedia.org/wiki/Kaaba.

busy slaughtering each other in Kabul, then we formed another group under the name of the Taliban to establish permanent peace. What atrocities did the Taliban commit in Afghanistan and in the wake of their defeat; what havoc did they wreck in Pakistan does not need to be mentioned because it is not a forgotten history of the past, but a contemporary story which we hear every now and then.

Today, our rulers and politicians are not tired of uttering, "This is not our war," but when they were adding fuel to the fire in Afghan Jihad by getting the CIA to publish the holy Quran, I wish any Munawar Hassan then, would emerge from somewhere and say don't drag the holy Quran into this conflict as it is not our war. When Kabul was being ruined and Afghanistan was being turned into a graveyard, I wish Imran Khan would sit-in protest and say, don't jump into this war, it is not our war. When the Taliban were hanging human bodies on trees, electric poles on the street, I wished Choudhry Nisar would make an appearance from here and there and yelled to keep away from this war as it is not our war. Had all this happened, we would not see such devastation around us. But we were busy enjoying the warmth of Peanuts in those days.

The original article was published on the DAWN Urdu website on December 24, 2013.[4]

Hassan Riza Changezi, "شیطان بزرگ اور سونگ کھلی کردانے" , DAWN Urdu, December 24, 2013,

https://www.dawnnews.tv/news/1000898.

19

Our high hopes of their constancy

With the start of the new year, terrorists have begun their celebration by drenching themselves in the blood of innocents across all four provinces of Pakistan; from Peshawar to Mastung and from Quetta to Karachi. Meanwhile, people are busy gathering and burying the scattered limbs of their beloved. It seems they bury their hopes too along with the dead bodies. In this vicious and terror-stricken atmosphere, people anxiously look up to the government and state agencies for some remedial response. The governmen officials, however, are busy doing their routine meetings followed always by a statement of condemnation. On the one hand, the terrorists are on a killing spree, and on the other hand, the government is trying hard to cajole their so-called spoilt brethren into peace talks.

In Quetta too, the new year began with a terrorist incident. In the neighbouring locality of Akhtar Abad, a bus carrying the pilgrims from the Punjab and KP (Khyber Pakhtunkhwa) provinces was hit by a suicide bomber.[1] The attack was a grim reminder that the terrorists could carry out their gruesome acts with impunity. The terrorist outfit Jaysh al-Islam, which had previously orchestrated several attacks on the Hazara community, claimed responsibility for the attack. People were still trying to come to terms with that horrific incident when on January 21st, a bus carrying pilgrims from the Hazara community was hit by a suicide bomber in Mastung district claiming more than 30 lives including those of women and children.[2] This time the notorious Lashkar-e-Jhangvi (LeJ) took responsibility for the attack.[3] The following morning when few of the community members headed to the graveyard to dig mass graves for the deceased; others including women, children and old members of the community, with the bodies of their beloved in coffins, gathered on Alamdar Road to stage a sit-in, in the frigidly cold weather.[4] They demanded that the government to start a complete crack down on the militant groups responsible for the attacks. Following

[1]Express News, " نے سال کے پہلے ہی دن کوئٹہ میں زائرین کی بس کے قریب بم دھماکہ دو افراد جہاں بحق متعدد زخمی ", Express News, January 01, 2014, https://www.express.pk/story/213296/.

[2]BBC News, "Bomb targets bus of Shia pilgrims in south-west Pakistan", BBC News, January 21, 2014, https://www.bbc.co.uk/news/world-asia-25832979.

[3]Syed Ali Shah, "Blast on bus kills 12 Shia pilgrims in Mastung," DAWN News, January 21, 2014, https://www.dawn.com/news/1081751.

[4]Shezad Baloch, "Mastung blast: Bereaved families stage sit-in along with the dead bodies", The Expres TRIBUNE, January 22, 2014, https://tribune.com.pk/story/661903/mastung-blast-bereaved-families-stage-sit-in-along-with-dead-bodies.

the incident, Prime Minister Nawaz Sharif sent a delegation under the supervision of the then interior minister, Chaudhary Nisar Ali Khan, who visited the provincial capital to hold negotiations with the members of the Hazara community and persuaded them to call off their protest.[5]

Following the string of these events, I was gripped with a feeling of déjà vu. I could recall how we had witnessed all of this before. Just last year, in the aftermath of the twin bomb blasts on Alamdar Road on January 10th , angered by the apathetic behaviour of the government and its state officials, the Hazara men, women and children with the coffins of their deceased had staged a similar sit-in. The then-Prime Minister, Raja Pervez Ashraf, had visited Quetta to offer his condolences to the bereaved and assured them of a stern response.[6] Later in the same year, upon his visit to Quetta, the newly elected Prime Minister Nawaz Sharif accompanied by General Ashfaq Ahmed Kiani and Director General of Inter-Services Intelligence (ISI) General Zaheer- ul- Islam, directed law enforcement agencies to act fast and immediately arrest the culprits who were involved in the killings of the Hazaras.[7] But the law enforcers turned a deaf ear to his directions, it seems, as atrocities of the terrorists continued

[5]IBID

[6]Shaan Khan, "Pakistani leader meets protesting families of bombing victims", CNN, January 13, 2013, https://edition.cnn.com/2013/01/13/world/asia/pakistan-blasts-bodies/index.html.

[7]The Express TRIBUNE, "Balochistan crises: Nawaz directs ISI, IB to catch Hazara town bombers", July 02, 2013, https://tribune.com.pk/story/571395/hazara-tragedy-nawaz-sharif-visits-quetta-to-discuss-security-situation.

unabated. A few months have passed since the incident, but the Hazara community is still living in a state of persistent fear. The law-and-order situation is rapidly deteriorating and is showing no signs of improvement in the near future. In the aftermath of the Mastung incident, when the members of the Hazara community were staging a sit-in, refusing to bury their dead and demanding swift action against the perpetrators, it seemed like a flashback of last year's incident. From the frigidly cold weather to the charred and mutilated dead bodies, from the wailing women and children to condemning statements of the government officials, from the .exhibition of support and solidarity to the hollow claims and fake promises, everything felt the same. If anything did seem different it was the change in personnel at the helm of the power. Nawaz Sharif instead of Raja Pervaiz Ashraf and Chaudhary Nisar Ali Khan instead of Rehman Malik as the country's prime ministers and interior ministers respectively were entrusted with the assignment of making false pledges to provide the Hazara community with a safer and peaceful future as part of their duties in the office. People have learned to take such promises with a pinch of salt, however.

Last year, after the Prime Minister Raja Ashraf had left, police raided some locations, a few suspects were rounded up, while a few were even killed in various hunt downs. But the merciless killings of the innocents have continued unabated. This has given credence to the impressions that the terrorists are either tolerated by the law enforcers or at worst they have their sympathizers and supporters within the official ranks.

121

No wonder why after carrying out their hideous acts, the assailants calmly stroll to nearby hotels to eat and drink without the fear of apprehension. It is fair to deduce then that the perpetrators of violence responsible for the death of innocent civilians are the same so-called patriotic and faithful folks affiliated with every terrorist outfit that is out there whether it is Laskar-e-Jhangvi, Jaysh al-Islam or Khalid bin Waleed Force. For the past 14 years, the ferocious massacres, that have taken place under the four successive governments and the persistent failure of authorities to apprehend the attackers, suggest that the authorities are either incompetent or possibly indifferent to this situation. This has laid credence to the belief that the government is unable to act against the terrorist outfits simply because they are involved with the killers, hand in glove.

It is easy to deduce then that in a country where law enforcement agencies, to avoid legal complications, constitute a private army or militia consisting of highly motivated and trained fighters;[8] where in the name of corridors of free passage, militants are sponsored and harboured; where criminals, for the sake of national interest, are given free hand to kill defenceless and innocent citizens after declaring them foreign agents; where police bow down to the terrorists instead of apprehending them; where a single phone call from higher up is enough to strike open the metal bars of the prison cell; where women and children are fed as mere fodders to the strategic

Shehzad Malik, "بلوچستان میں سکورٹی گروپس کو غیر مؤثر کرنے کا فیصلہ", BBC Urdu, December 28, 2013, Https://www.bbc.com/urdu/pakistan/2013/12/131227_balochistan_secur ity_groups_zis.

assets of the country; there are people like Asif Ali Zardari, Nawaz Sharif, Rehman Malik, Chaudry Nisar Ali Khan and Dr. Abdul Malik (the Chief Minister of Balochistan), who can offer no more than lip service to protect the citizenry and yet surround themselves with an army of guards.

In an interview with the Jang newspaper Quetta, published on December 4th, 2013, the president of Pakistan Medical Association Balochistan Dr. Sultan Tareen made some horrific revelations about the kidnappings for ransom of doctors. According to him, a famous doctor from Chaman who was abducted for ransom, was held hostage in a house where he happened to overhear the conversation between kidnappers. Apparently, the kidnappers had spent a whopping 6 million to bribe the law enforcers designated at various check posts. Surprisingly, in the early hours of the day of Mastung incident, the police had raided a house on Sariab Road to free Ramesh Kumar, a businessman who had been abducted for ransom a few days earlier. During the raid, three kidnappers were killed in the police shootout. The following day, the spokesman for Jaysh al-Islam, the group responsible for carrying out the suicide bombings in Akhtar Abad, called the offices of print and electronic media and claimed that the three criminals killed were their fellow mujahideen and demanded the government for the recovery of their dead bodies. Without a shred of a doubt, had the kidnappers complied with the police orders and released the businessman, there would have been no need for the shoot-out. This is not an isolated incident, such stories in Balochistan, particularly Quetta, are aplenty. The law enforcement agencies turn a blind eye to the abductors as they get paid by them. So, the kidnappers operate with complete impunity. These kidnappers belong to the same patriotic and faithful groups mentioned earlier who easily manage to pass through the security checkpoints. There are never any complaints registered against them in powerless police stations.

The government's persistent failure to prevent these attacks raise plenty of questions. Would the elected Prime Minister and chief minister of the province[9] be able to fulfil the aspirations of the people? Would the government be able to provide the public with the basic right to live, as guaranteed by the constitution of this country? Should the Hazara community ever trust Chaudhary Nisar for his promise of bringing the culprits to justice and restoring peace in the province? Can our mothers be optimistic of their children's future and that they would never fall prey to the barbarism of the extremists?

People have every right to ask the government about the delayed crackdown on the terrorists. To keep this hydra of terrorism alive, how many more innocent lives will be scarified? Perhaps the government is waiting for the pull out of NATO troops from Afghanistan thus this theatre of absurd might just be a ruse to keep the terrorists active.

The original article was first published on DAWN Urdu website on January 31, 2014.[10]

[9]Mohammed Kazim, "هزاره والے کے لیے دہشت گردی نہیں سکتے نہار", BBC Urdu, January 24, 2014, Https://www.bbc.com/urdu/pakistan/2014/01/140123_mustung_sit_in_ended_rwa.

[10]Hassan Riza Changezi, "ہم کان سے دعائیں ہاہیں", DAWN Urdu, January 31, 2014, https://www.dawnnews.tv/news/1001918.\

20

Opportunistic Flip-Floppers in Pakistani Media

Two female neighbours were engaged in a heated argument. They had their sleeves rolled up, mouths foamed, and were making obscene hand gestures, all the while accusing each other of being unchaste. Revealing each other's dirty secrets, one shouted, "I am not too dumb to figure out your affair with the milkman." The other immediately responded, "You are not so chaste either. One does not get free vegetables from the vendor for no reason." They continued their belligerent rant. Having overheard this, a neighbouring gentleman asked his wife, "Why don't you intervene and end the dispute?" The wife replied, "Why should I? They are doing a good job exposing each other."

The current Pakistani media landscape presents the same view. Since the assassination attempt on senior journalist Hamid Mir in Karachi, the media especially TV journalists have launched a vicious campaign defaming and exposing one another. The whole episode is quite enlightening for the ignorant lot like me. The unending blame game amidst accusations of treason indicates that the media and TV channels appear to be following the footsteps of their political counterparts. The general perception about the Pakistani media industry is that it has never been impartial.

I can recall my days as a mass communication student, where one day our professor, during his lecture about ethics in journalism, said, "A journalist ought to be impartial." Yet, only in his next breath he immediately negated his statement and said, "This is next to impossible." Over the next many years, I struggled to fathom the reason for having something taught in theory which then cannot be put to practice.

Some of my friends would occasionally poke fun at my profession, saying that even though it is the police who are notorious bribe-takers, the journalists are a notch above. I, personally, never took these jibes too seriously. The sprouting of new TV channels in Pervez Musharraf's reign, however, played a significant role in changing that, by unveiling the true face of journalism in Pakistan. What seemed like a joke yesterday became an undeniable truth. Many journalists whose writings and reporting I was a fan of, failed to meet my expectations once they frequented my TV screen. I soon realized that I had incorrectly put them on high pedestals.

Undoubtedly, journalists are not divorced from the earthly biases that the rest of us hold. They too have their own preferences. Likewise, media groups across the world carry a specific agenda. They work endlessly to attain their objectives, which among many other things include, the acquisition of power and influence alongside earning the highest possible revenues. While carrying out their duties, however, they maintain certain etiquettes such that an audience would never get the impression that they might be influencing his opinions. In Pakistan, however, things are different. Here the practice is carried in such an absurd and explicit manner that it is easy to deduce whether the journalist is favouring or is hostile towards a specific group. Like politicians who switch political loyalties at whims, the journalists switch channels. Such journalists change their ideologies with changing media houses to meet the agenda set by the new employers. And with that, their priorities change alongside their beliefs.

Media is regarded as the fourth pillar of the state not just because it serves as a bridge between people and other three pillars, namely, judiciary, executive, and legislature, of the state, but also performs its part as a watchdog. To fulfil this significant task, it is essential for the media to remain impartial. On the contrary, many journalists in our country are accused of serving the government of the day or intelligence agencies in return for favours. A journalist who has the greatest access to the said duo is believed to be the most well-informed. Journalists are opinion-makers for they possess the ability to influence public opinion owing to their extensive knowledge of current affairs. Regrettably, in Pakistan, many media houses and prominent journalists regard themselves as kingmakers. They believe they are powerful enough to elevate anyone to fame or bring down anyone they disdain. It is, therefore, that currently, they are in the business of making and breaking governments. The governments, state institutions, and politicians are as much to be blamed as journalists for this trend. A 2013 report by the media commission, had details of accusations on journalists, the topmost of which was the kickbacks journalists and media houses received from politicians to get favourable coverage for themselves and fake news and propaganda against their opponents. It is an open secret now that most Pakistani media persons use their influence to force, threaten, and even blackmail people to get their work done. Favours and rewards from the government and state agencies in the form of land, cash and foreign tours are well known too. Journalists exposing their rivals, labelling them as traitors, or uploading some video evidence of their rival's true characters on YouTube and Facebook are common, too. In given circumstances, people are confused as to who should they believe in, those who regard themselves as true patriots and label their rivals as traitors or foreign agents, or those who deem any criticism against them as a conspiracy against democracy, which also threatens freedom of expression and independence of journalism.

Just the other day, in a campaign against the government, some apparently well-informed anchors were sharing the assets and bank account details of the Sharif family in a manner that would lead most to believe that a charge-sheet was being filed against the ruling government. Then events took a drastic turn, with the media then switching its guns towards Hamid Mir and Jang Group. Alongside the usual accusations of both being traitors and foreign agents, some even went ahead by claiming that the Jang Group had especially paid a hitman of the notorious Lashkar-e-Jhangvi group to kill Wali Babar, a reporter of their own channel. On the other hand, Hamid Mir and his employer, the Jang Group, claimed that they were being targeted for highlighting the plight of Balochistan, the news itself shatters the myth of freedom of expression in the country. Contrary to the claims, people of Balochistan have always complained about the lack of coverage of the provincial affairs by the mainstream Pakistani media.

The issue of Balochistan is not a recent one. The most recent wave of unrest and resistance started in 2006 when the senior Baloch Leader Nawab Akbar Bugti was killed in an operation carried by the country's military. In the days following the incident, none of the so-called patriotic and outspoken journalists in the Pakistani media industry could muster up the courage to condemn the attack or call it unlawful and detrimental for the country. In contrast, they not only referred to the incident as lawful in their shows- which to them further strengthened the writ of the government- but also played host to ministers of the dictators' cabinet and did their best to justify the brutal killing. This irresponsible attitude of Pakistani media was once again on display in 2007, in the wake of the Lal Masjid incident in Islamabad. One can recall how initially the media played its part in pushing the government for an operation against the baton-bearing, burka-clad female students along with their armed to teeth male counterparts. After the government launched an operation that freed the Lal Masjid and Jamia Hafsa from the hold of the extremists, all the media, in a drastic change of stance, started accusing the government of killing the innocent students. People were confused whether the media was right before or after the operation. The dismal performance of the media can also be assessed from its inability to cover the dreadful sectarian violence that engulfed the entire country, Quetta in particular, during the reign of the dictator General Pervez Musharraf. Nor did they possess the nerves to name the terrorists and their supporters, involved in the sectarian violence. Our renowned journalists instead, found solace in glorifying Taliban and Al-Qaeda by tagging them Mardani Hur (brave warriors) and hailed Usama bin Laden as their hero. They are still found expressing their longing for the Taliban's rule in the Islamic Republic of Pakistan and keep desiring a rule that viciously kills innocent people. Such is the extent of their hypocrisy that these journalists have chosen to keep their lips sealed on the killings of innocent people by the Taliban and their allies. Instead, with their pale faces and feeble disposition, they appear to be apologetic in their live programs. They are also the pioneers of the nomenclature of Good and Bad Taliban's, those involved in slitting the throats of the Afghans being the former while the ones wreaking havoc domestically being the latter. As far as groups like Lashkar-e-Jhangvi are concerned, the journalists still seem to be at crossroads whether to call them

Mardani Hur or terrorists. They have yet to determine, it seems, whether Lashkar-e-Jhangvi is killing us or our enemies.

According to an estimate, there are 150 TV channels running in Pakistan. Most of these are entertainment channels that broadcast programs of various genres including movies, dramas, and music. The number of news channels is around 20, each claiming to be "The First" in breaking the news or the only credible sourced news outlet. In the mad race of staying ahead of their rivals and earning greater TRP, none of them seems to care for the desecration of ethics in their profession. If such is the attitude of the torchbearers of credible news providers, then one cannot find a fault in the blind followers. That old adage sums it up well, "If gold rusts, what shall iron do." I wish our journalists followed the standards set by their counterparts in the west, who have rightly been deemed as the founders of journalism and its ethics. Ironically, it is India- which we regard as our greatest enemy- which we try to imitate. Sensationalism in talk shows, yelling at the guests, and provoking them for a scuffle, are things we have learned from them. There are, however, some credible investigative journalists in India who would go to lengths trying to search and report the truth. The example of one Tehelka.com is apt, it is responsible for publishing an investigative report on the 2002 Gujrat riots. Although completely operated by the Hindus, the web-based media brought to light not just the atrocities of a Hindu extremist organization, Bajrang Dal, but also brought forth the role of Narendra Modi (the then Chief Minister of

Gujarat and the incumbent Prime Minister of India) in the carnage, with such sheer audacity that makes one wish that our valorous journalists could also emulate.

With an abundance of news channels and users' discretion in the selection of channels, the quality of journalism should have naturally improved. To stay ahead of the competition and get the audiences glued to TV screens more, the focus should have been laid on the quality, credibility, and presentation of the news. Highlighting the social issues, the government should have been made aware of ordinary men's problems. Programs should have been aired to help equality and harmony prevail in the country. On the contrary, to improve their ratings and increase their ad revenues, the news channels have adhered to creating sensationalism and gross exaggeration of news to the extent that could put some of the evening newspapers to shame. Some channels use such a horrific signature tune in their breaking news that makes one's blood freeze. Fake news is at the full display when vehicular silencer's sound or explosion of a gas cylinder are presented as a bomb blast so as to create unnecessary hype. Not for once, have they apologized for any of such incorrect news items, even though the code of conduct of PEMRA (Pakistan Electronic Media Regulatory Authority) obliges them to do so.

Witnessing their morning shows, it is hard to confirm if one is watching a news channel at all. Clown anchors dressed in vibrant and colourful clothes are seen prating, giving make-up tips, sharing cooking recipes, and dancing. According to the rules of PEMRA, news and entertainment are two different categories of channels, but the owners have incorporated so much entertainment in their news channels that it is difficult to differentiate between the two.

A large airtime of the majority of news channels is dedicated to the shows that present historical re-enactment. There is no harm in the dramatization per se, but their presentation makes it look rather unauthentic. It seems more like a bid to fill the gaps in the transmission. Often in the garb of highlighting societal evils, people's lives are interfered in a manner wherein the elements of force, harassment, threats, blackmailing, and sensationalism are on full display. In some of the shows, the host behaves more like an authoritative police officer who would not mind fettering his guests. In 2012, only after the public outcry, a female anchor of one such show was suspended by the channel for interfering in people's private lives. The lady in question, an erstwhile actress, professed later that her program was a drama where paid actors performed as real-life people. Despite the magnitude of the scandal, she did not remain unemployed for too long as soon another news channel hired her services. Currently, she is busy grappling between supernatural forces and learned babas. Who knows, one day she might confess that supernatural forces and babas were also actors working on the payroll of the channel.

Another trendy show seen across almost every TV channel is the quibble laden stand-up comedy. Such shows contain a number of stage actors who enchant the audience with humorous jibes and witty dialogues. The language used in most of such shows is Punjabi which for people in other provinces is difficult if not impossible to understand. It is only natural for denizens of other provinces to believe that the media favours Punjab more than any other province and it is there that they get most of the ad revenues from. The only question that looms here is whether or not such programs deserve to be aired at all, amidst the frequency of tragedy and abundance of wailing mourners in the country.

Moving on to prime time, deemed the most significant part of TV transmission. Running from 8 to 11 o'clock at night, it is in these hours that TV channels run their most important programs, from talk shows to discussions to news analysis. Usually, senior and informed journalists or anchors share their information with the audience. In the midst of their analysis in such talk shows, the hosts, at times, challenge their guests in a manner that resembles the dialogues of one Moula Jatt movie. To a layman, it might look like a ploy to induce some humour in the otherwise tedious show. In the prime-time hour, one gets to witness excessive boasting, vilification, and accusation in the name of "talk shows". They are replete with such amusing content that puts the entertainment to shame. These shows have their own popularity gauge, the more slanderous the discourse, the more popular the show. The hosts too do their best in turning arguments to scuffle by stirring up controversies among the guests. The objective of the host, it seems, is to not only help the popularity of the show- which means more revenues in advertisements- but also help them win a celebrity status. Only a handful of anchors are exceptions who are civil to their guests and talk about real issues in their programs.

More recently the journalists and their employers have been found indulged in demeaning and exposing one another. Seeing them, one is forced to wonder if all the problems of the country have been solved and peace prevails through its length; Taliban and their allies- the sectarian groups- have corrected their ways; law and order in Karachi have improved; sectarian violence and the issue of mutilated bodies dumped in the province of Balochistan have been resolved; inflation has been controlled; the standard of living of the common man has improved; load shedding has become a thing of the past; a number of suicides case due to poverty has dropped, and in short, the Islamic Republic of Pakistan presents a picture of heaven. In contrast, the problems haven't contracted an inch. Politicians and religious leaders have also joined this web of conflicts between journalists and various media groups. Seeing their opportunity in this conflict, they are openly asking for a boycott of Geo and Jang Groups. There is no doubt that the attack on Hamid Mir is condemnable on every ground. It is the law enforcers' duty to apprehend and ascertain their motives. Meanwhile, the vicious game of accusations between journalists and TV channels is not a good omen for the future of journalism in Pakistan. What happened to Hamid Mir may happen to other journalists too, after all, Pakistan is regarded as one of the most dangerous countries for journalists, as many have lost their lives in the line of duty. In the circumstances, the attack on Hamid Mir may well be a signal for other journalists. If they don't take the incident seriously and do not refrain from the petty mudslinging on one another, it wouldn't be possible for them to perform their duties fearlessly. Sadly enough, owing to the fuss created by the lawyers, politicians, and religious leaders with their participation in the act, the real issue has been pushed to the background. The constant hurls of accusations and counteraccusations have got the public divided too, which some journalists and media groups see as an opportune moment and are using it to their advantage. The conflict is being heavily utilized for their monetary gains while some journalists and politicians have only joined in to settle scores with the Jang Group.

The need of the hour is for the journalists and media houses to review and chart their code of conduct. They have to agree to a joint code of ethics for the entire Pakistani media so their profession is purged of any political clout which can then raise the quality of journalism in the country.

June 02, 2014

21

Terrorist Filter Plant

In the evening of 8th June, after raiding the
international airport in Karachi, when some
bad Taliban were busy spraying bullets;[1]
simultaneously, in the border town of Taftan,
in Balochistan, some good Taliban were targeting
pilgrims using shells and grenades.,[2,3] Tehreek-i-
Taliban Pakistan claimed responsibility for the attack
on the airport in Karachi[4] while for the Taftan episode,
Jaish-ul-Islam took the credit.[5] Two days later, on the
10th of June, when the interior minister, Chaudhary

---

[1]Imran Ayub, "کراچی حملہ کب اور کیسے ہوا؟", DAWN Urdu, June 11, 2014,
https://www.dawnnews.tv/news/1005711.

[2]Mohammed Kazim, "10 مسافروں سمیت 25 شیعہ زائرین ہلاک", BBC Urdu, June 09, 2014,
https://www.bbc.com/urdu/pakistan/2014/06/140608_shia_bus_attack_t
aftan_sa.

[3]BBC News, "Shia pilgrims killed in Pakistan", BBC News, June 08, 2014,
https://www.bbc.co.uk/news/world-asia-27757856.

[4]BBC News, "Taliban claim deadly attack on Karachi airport", BBC News,
June 09, 2014, https://www.bbc.co.uk/news/world-asia-27758029.

[5]Syed Ali Shah, "PM orders action as Taftan bombing death toll reaches 24",
DAWN News, June 09, 2014,
https://www.dawn.com/news/1111403.

Nisar was briefing the national assembly on the Karachi incident, at the very same time, the news of the attack on the base of Pakistan's Airport Security Force (ASF), located Karachi international airport, was spreading like wildfire.[6] Not long ago, the government and Taliban were busy exchanging gifts and pleasantries where the latter was generously presenting the dead bodies of innocents as souvenirs, the former was reciprocating by releasing their notoriously deadly prisoners as a good will gesture.[7,8] Seemingly, the two were betrothed and a formal engagement ceremony was all that was left. Taliban, contrary to its counterpart, proved to be shockingly cunning. They wanted to have their cake and eat it too. They accepted their newly freed brethren but didn't keep to their end of the bargain. The synchronicity of the twin attacks on the Karachi airport, and the assault on pilgrims in Taftan indicate that the attacks might have been planned by both the good and the bad Taliban together. When the poor women and children were being targeted and their wails were piercing the ears of the sky in Taftan, the Pakistani media was busy covering the airport attack in Karachi.

While addressing a session in the national assembly, the interior minister did mention the Taftan

[6]DAWN News, "TTP claims attack on Karachi ASF camp", DAWN News, June 10, 2014,
https://www.dawn.com/news/1111791.

[7]DAWN Urdu, "حکومت کا مزید 13 طالبان قیدی رہا کرنے کا اعلان", DAWN Urdu, April 05, 2014,
https://www.dawnnews.tv/news/1003846.

[8]ABC News, "Pakistan announces release of Taliban prisoners to help ongoing peace talks", ABC News, April 06, 2014,
https://www.abc.net.au/news/2014-04-06/an-pakistan-announces-release-of-taliban-prisoners/5370426.

incident as well. In his remarks, he said, "Owing to its distance and remoteness of the area, the government is struggling to provide security for this highway". He even complained, "At the risk of financial loss, the government has offered to provide flight facilities to pilgrims, but no one is ready to avail the service because tour operators and transport companies are profiteering through the existing land routes". Ironically, as the honourable minister was briefing the house about the flight facilities for the pilgrims, Karachi airport was once again under attack with all its flights suspended.[9]

The honourable minister was right to remark that pilgrims need not travel through the Quetta-Taftan route as his government cannot provide them any security. But would he be able to name a single place in the country where people are safe, where mosques, imambargahs, churches and other religious places are safe? If the answer is in the negative, would it be fair then to bar people from going to such places? If schools are bombed and their buses are targeted, would it then be fair to stop them from getting education? Office workers too are targeted on a daily basis, then should we suggest they avoid going to their offices? Public places including bazars, markets and residential areas are not safe from terrorists hit list either, is it wise then to restrict people to their homes?

As the wise say, if the water is contaminated from the source, it is no use to send it anywhere. With the

[9] Afp/ Sohail Khattak/ Tahir Khan/ Faraz Khan/ web desk/Saad Hassan, "TTP claims attack on ASF hostel in Karachi", The Express TRIBUNE, June 08, 2014,

Https://tribune.com.pk/story/719242/four-security-personnel-injured-in-attack-on-karachi-airport.

exception of the Punjab, more or less, all other areas in Pakistan frequently face threats of terrorism. It has affected all and sundry, from security personnel to a common man. In the region from Karachi to Quetta and all the way to Khyber Pakhtunkhwa (KPK), the soil is soaked with the blood of innocent children, men and women. Carrying out attacks through using bombs has become a child's play. Terrorists have no fear whatsoever of anybody or anything. Law enforcement agencies have completely failed in combating terrorism. Despite having prior knowledge, the state officials fail to stop the attack, and instead indulge in a never-ending cycle of blame game.

In recent years, after every terrorist act, government officials, political parties and civil societies release a ritualistic statement; and security measures are tightened for a short span of time; some assailants are arrested in a normative hunt down and some are killed in encounters. Eventually, people start going on with their daily business, thanks to our short memory span. This is the ideal time for terrorists to plot new attacks using new strategies. They plan on trying new tactics, find loopholes in security measures and at the very first opportunity they get, they execute their plans with utmost devotion. Law enforcement and government agencies, on the contrary, lack this sincerity. Government officials are more interested in completing their tenure and filling their coffers. With the law enforcement agencies in a deep slumber. For obvious reasons, this is no more than a lack of sincerity and desire, on their part, to solve the issues.

It is completely futile to argue there was no

terrorist attack post 9/11 on American soil. Same is true for many other countries across Europe, that were able to prevent such incidents by timely monitoring and arresting people suspected of carrying out terrorist attacks. Needless to say, that instead of hunting down terrorist individuals or lone actors, they focused on eliminating the terrorist organisations; found ways of restricting their foreign aids; and worked on rebuilding their intelligence agencies. They have placed combating terrorism at the top of their national security policies.

Every state has an obligation to protect its citizens from all sorts of violence. Confining them to their homes is no solution. If the state is determined in ending terrorism, then it needs to take some very firm decisions and start cracking down on all the terrorist organisations indiscriminately. To help build a better Pakistan, it is about time for government and state officials to create counter terrorism strategies with no distinction between good and bad Taliban. The proverbial milk has not been spilt yet; but before it does, the government needs to put an end to this whole drama of exchanging gifts, playing hide and seek and peace talks. For rooting out the poison of terrorism, it is imperative to stop sources of impurities. Putting up filter plants at every nook and corner would be a cosmetic exercise.

The original article was published in DAWN Urdu website on June 15, 2014.[10]

---

[10]Hassan Riza Changezi, "دہشت گردی کا فلٹر پلانٹ", DAWN Urdu, June 15, 2014, https://www.dawnnews.tv/news/1005819/15jun14-you-wont-be-spared-next-time-riza-changezi-aq

22

Iraq and Syria on the Brink of Destruction

With each passing day, the situation in Syria and Iraq is rapidly deteriorating. When President Barak Obama announced the withdrawal of American troops from Iraq in December 2011,[1] he said, in a promising tone, that the US was leaving behind a country with a sovereign, stable, and self-reliant government. Despite the complete pull out of the US troops from Iraq, the country has failed to maintain peace and has witnessed continued violence from the terrorist groups. However, with fast growing instability in the region, a vicious war seems quite imminent. Neighbouring Syria is experiencing a civil war for the past couple of years. Some estimates put the numbers of casualties as high as 120,000 with

[1] Mark Landler, "U.S. Troops to Leave Iraq by Year's End, Obama Says", New York Times, October 21, 2011,

Https://www.nytimes.com/2011/10/22/world/middleeast/president-obama-announces-end-of-war-in-iraq.html.

another 2.5 million seeking refuge in neighbouring states.[2] The rebel groups battling the government are believed to be affiliated with Al-Qaida and Islamic State (ISIS) that are aspiring to establish an independent caliphate over Iraq and Syria. Daesh, also known as Islamic State in Iraq and Syria (ISIS) or Islamic State of Iraq and Levant (ISIL) has thousands of local and foreign fighters among its ranks, according to a report published by BBC Urdu.[3]

At the same time, Hassan Nasrullah, leader of the Lebanese Shi'ite militant group Hezbollah, has publicly acknowledged his party's involvement against the rebels in Syria.[4] Al Arabia, a Dubai based media group, has accused Iran of using thousands of Afghan refugees in Iran as mercenaries to fight rebels in Syria by offering them financial incentives, according to a report published on their Persian website.[5] Meanwhile, the Afghan refugees living in Iran have blamed Iranian officials for coercing them to participate in the war in Syria or face deportation back to Afghanistan.[6]

[2]"Total Persons of Concern," Syria Regional Refugee Response, UNHCR, last updated on August 14, 2020,
https://data2.unhcr.org/en/situations/syria.

[3]BBC, "آئی ایس آئی ایس یاداعش کس کا نام ہے؟", BBC Urdu, June 12, 2014,
https://www.bbc.com/urdu/world/2014/06/140612_isis_profile_fz.shtml.

[4]Iran Urdu Radio, "سید حسن نصر اللہ کا خطاب", Iran Urdu Radio: IRIB World Service, March 30, 2014,
http://urduold.ws.irib.ir/2010-06-28-08-41-22/interviews/item/49913-

[5]Maria Shehadah, "ایران پچیم یان افغان را با ماہیانہ ۵۰۰ دلار روانہ سوریہ کند", Al-Arabia Farsi, June 8, 2014,
https://farsi.alarabiya.net/fa/middle-east/2014/06/08/

[6]Mehdi Jedinia and Noor Zahid, "Iran Sending afghan Refugees to Fight in Syria", Voice of America, January 29, 2016,
https://www.voanews.com/world-news/middle-east-dont-use/iran-sending-afghan-refugees-fight-syria

According to a report by the Wall Street Journal, the office of Grand Shi'ite Afghan religious leader, Ayatollah Mohaqiq Kabuli, located in the Iranian city of Qom, has confirmed that the Islamic Revolutionary Guard Corps (IRGC) and other Iranian officials are making every effort to convince Afghan youth to go and fight for Syrian government[7] by offering them legal residence and school registration for their children among other incentives (just a reminder- children of Afghan refugees living are not allowed school registration in Iran). Reportedly, the office of the Ayatollah Kabuli has chosen to avoid a public stance lately and has not attended the funeral processions of Afghans refugees killed in Syria.

Although Iran has strongly dismissed these allegations, a close look at the fast-changing scenario in the Middle East particularly in Iraq, and the statements made by the regional and international leaders, will tell that a full-fledged war is just around the corner.

In the past few days, ISIS militants seized control of Mosul,[8] a strategically significant Iraqi city near the borders of Turkey and Syria. The battle, which lasted no longer than five days, claimed a high number of casualties and forced an estimated half a million residents to flee and take refuge in neighbouring areas. Sources claim that after Mosul, ISIS leaders are

---

[7]Farnaz Fassihi, "Iran Pays Afghans to Fight for Assad", The Wall Street Journal, May 22, 2014,
https://www.wsj.com/articles/iran-recruiting-afghan-refugees-to-fight-for-regime-in-syria-1400197482?tesla=y.

[8]BBC, "موصل پر آئی ایس آئی ایس کا کنٹرول، ایمرجنسی لگانے کی درخواست", BBC Urdu, June 10, 2014,
https://www.bbc.com/urdu/world/2014/06/140610_iraq_mosul_isis_control_rh.shtml.

planning to gain control of other Iraqi cities including Baghdad and Karbala.[9] Following the advances made by ISIS in Iraq, Iran has announced it will send troops to support the Iraqi government if needed. According to news sources, Iranian President Hassan Rouhani is considering the possibility of cooperating with his rival the United States,[10] to defeat the militant groups. However, this could not be confirmed independently. According to the Wall Street Journal, Iran would not hesitate to work with the US to tackle ISIS as they both share a common interest in defeating ISIS in Iraq, however, in case of Syria, their choices diverge significantly.[11]

In a June 12th report, the Los Angeles Times says that the Obama administration has hinted it will consider a direct military action[12] in the face of rising threats posed by the Sunni militant groups which are likely to trigger a sectarian war in the Middle East. A

---

[9]Jim Sciutto, Nic Robertson and Laura Smith-Spark, "Recordings: ISIS promises more fightings in more Iraqi cities", CNN, June 12, 2014,

https://edition.cnn.com/2014/06/11/world/meast/iraq-violence/.

[10]Martin Chulov, "Iran sends troops into Iraq to aid fight against Isis militants", The Guardian, June 14, 2014,

https://www.theguardian.com/world/2014/jun/14/iran-iraq-isis-fight-militants-nouri-maliki.

[11]Farnaz Fassihi, "Iran's Deploys Forces to Fight al-Qaeda-Inspired Militants in Iraq", The Wall Street Journal, June 12, 2014,
https://www.wsj.com/articles/iran-deploys-forces-to-fight-al-qaeda-inspired-militants-in-iraq-iranian-security-sources-1402592470.

[12]Paul Richter and David S. Cloud, "Obama weights direct action against insurgents in Iraq", Los Angeles Times, June 12, 2014,

https://www.latimes.com/world/middleeast/la-fg-obama-iraq-20140613-story.html#page=1.

call by Iraq's most revered Shia cleric, Ayatollah Al-Sistani upon his followers to join security forces in the fight against ISIS[13] clearly offers an insight on the gravity of the situation in the region. Meanwhile, there are reports about a large number of Kurdish fighters who have entered the northern oil rich city of Kirkuk.[14] They have allegedly taken control of this regional oil hub and its surrounding areas in an attempt to defend their territory from the Islamic State. The recent advancements have raised the possibility of deep ethnic and sectarian tensions in the region which not only threatens to drag the neighbouring states of Iran, Turkey, Saudi Arabia, Syria and Jordan into a bitter conflict, but also can impact other Muslim countries across the globe.

A number of studies have been carried out on the demographic division of Iraq in recent years. In June 2006, when the Iraq civil war was at its peak, Ralph Peters in his article under the title of "Blood Brothers"[15] published in the "US Armed Forces Journal" described the borders of many Middle Eastern countries including Iraq as the world's most unnatural. Mr. Peters' radical solution for Iraq, includes redrawing of

---

[13]Al Jazeera, "Iraq cleric issues call to arms against ISIL", Al Jazeera, June 14, 2014,
https://www.aljazeera.com/news/middleeast/2014/06/iraq-cleric-issues-call-arms-against-isil-2014613125518278210.html.

[14]Fazel Hawramy and Peter Beaumont, "Iraqi Kurdish forces take Kirkuk as Isis sets its sights on Baghdad", The Guardian,

https://www.theguardian.com/world/2014/jun/12/iraq-isis-kirkuk-baghdad-kurdish-government.

[15]Ralph Peters, "Blood borders", Armed Forces Journal, June 1, 2006, http://armedforcesjournal.com/blood-borders/.

boundaries of Iraq and several other Middle Eastern countries in-line with their ethnic and religious homogeneity. Referring to the current borders as the ultimate source of conflicts, he further recommends redrawing territorial boundaries of Iraq, Iran, Turkey and Syria to form an independent Kurdistan. Likewise, the readjustment of the Shia majority areas in Saudi Arabia and Iraq would result in the formation of an independent Shia Arab state that will also include some parts of Shia majority areas of Iran. The remaining three Sunni majority provinces of Iraq could ultimately choose to merge with Syria, he suggests. The author declares Pakistan as an example of an unnatural state[16] and further argues that some areas between Pakistan and Iran should be readjusted to form an independent Baluchistan, while Pakistan's Pashtun region might choose to unite with their brethren in Afghanistan. Similarly, Herat province in Afghanistan and its surrounding areas might choose to merge with Iran. According to the writer, boundary revisions respectful of people's aspirations might seem impossible at present but in due course and only after bloodshed on a mass scale, birth of more just and natural borders is a possibility. In his ending remarks, the writer expressed his wish in these words, "If we could reshuffle the borders by waving a magic wand, we would preferably choose to do so".[17]

Undeniably, Iran and the Arab states, particularly Saudi Arabia, are to be blamed for a large share of the mess we see in the Middle East. Their ambitious

[16]Ibid.

[17]Ibid.

strategic policies to dominate the region has contributed to the worsening situation. Having said that, there are other external forces at play who have fixated their eyes over the natural resources this region houses. If an immediate resolution to this conflict is not found, an inevitable war would not spare any nation in the region and even beyond.

The original essay was published on DAWN News website on June 19, 2014.[18]

[18]Hasan Riza Changezi, "عراق اور شام: تباہی کے دہانے پر", Dawn News, June 19, 2014, https://www.dawnnews.tv/news/1006023.

23

Quds Day! An Iranian Agenda

" Shias do not have the right to live in Palestine. We are on our way to establishing a Salafi state. Palestine is the best region for a Salafi state in the Middle East and I stand for a Salafi Palestine."

This is part of the statement of Mahmoud Abbas, the President of the Palestinian Authority, which he gave on June 2, 2014, and which Iranian media published as headlines. In the statement, Abbas further claimed that he had been in talks with Hamas over the issue and that he hoped the country would come out of this quagmire soon. In the concluding section of this report by the Shiite News, there is a reference to the United States Secretary of State, John Kerry, who is alleged to have said, "I am happy Hamas is a Salafi group who could help bring an end to the resistance movement in Palestine".

Yes, he is the same Mahmoud Abbas who assumed the leadership of Palestine Liberation Organization

(PLO) after the demise of Yasser Arafat on November 11, 2004; and became the President of Palestinian authority on January 15, 2005. Hamas, mentioned here in this statement, is the same organization that, with the support from the United States, fought numerous bloody battles with PLO in order to occupy the Gaza strip. More currently, this is the same Hamas which has been sharing perks and privileges of government with Mahmoud Abbas for a long time. Not only Iran provides patronage to Hamas but also rolled out the red carpet when hosting its leaders Khaled Mashal and Ismail Haniyeh as it has done previously to Gulbuddin Hekmatyar and the leadership of Al-Qaida. On the one hand, in this affair or strategic calculations and political bargaining, we seem to be brainlessly dancing to the tunes of others and we overreact in our affection for Mahmoud Abbas and Hamas. Both PLO and Hamas seem to have abandoned their quests for an independent Palestine and they seem to be complacent with their respective rule over what remains of the territories divided along sectarian lines which they have been pushing into a civil war like that of Iraq and Syria's.

The subject of this article is Quds Day which I believe is not a spiritual affair and which, instead is an Iranian political agenda. The day is celebrated following a decree issued by Iranian supreme leader Ayatollah Khomeini in 1979. Those were the days when the Palestinian intifada was in its culmination to liberate their land from Israel. The day is celebrated to express solidarity with the Palestinian intifada. Today, 35 years have passed since the decree was issued and

25 years have elapsed from Khomeini's demise. In the meanwhile, the Palestinian leadership has abandoned the armed struggle and has engaged in the peace process with Israel for more than a decade. Only because Iran has been using the day as a political agenda, therefore, on this day, thousands of people come out to protest on the street in Iran and Iranian diaspora communities around the world to celebrate the day to show their affiliation with their motherland. There are few people in our society who have turned this political agenda into a religious festival. They exploit the religious sentiments of people and lure them to attend the procession to expect a reward from Allah.

An interesting point is that adhering to a deceased Mujtahid is forbidden according to the injunction of Shia Islam. What else can it be termed other than advancing the Iranian political agenda when they are using the cover of the 1979 Khomeini fatwa even after 25 years of his demise? They are exploiting religious sentiments and endangering the lives of innocent youth by dragging them to unnecessary street protests under volatile security circumstances. To accomplish this old Iranian agenda and in order to turn Pakistan into a battleground for SaudiIran proxy war and to invigorate sectarian conflicts, an unnecessary drama was staged in 2010 to show solidarity to Palestine. The organizers of this drama were those clerics who had returned from religious seminaries of Iran, and who did not care to conceal their reckless disregard even if Quetta is pushed to burn in a bloody sectarian conflict. They keep glorifying martyrdoms for youth but themselves they won't step out of their homes without a squad of armed security guards. They hold processions in support of Lebanon and Palestine as commanded by Iran. They don't shy away from losing hundreds of youths in the bombings while protesting for Palestine and Lebanon but fail to explain why Palestinians, Lebanese, and Iranians remained silent during the last 15 years as we have been going through hell like situation? I wish an "oppressed Palestinian" had offered her/his condolences to the bereaved family members who lost their loved ones while protesting for Palestine. Our pro-Iran clerics have failed to explain why Shia Iran would not provide safe sanctuary to those fleeing persecution. Aren't persecuted Shia Muslims seeking refuge in non-Muslim countries in Europe and elsewhere? Why haven't our clerics objected to the inhuman and racist treatment of Hazaras in Iran where they are called names as Afghani Khar (i.e., Afghans, the donkeys) Khawari, Barbari, and dirty. Why is this unfair racist treatment met out to Hazaras exclusively whereas other Afghan refugees who share their ethnic roots with Iran are embraced as one of their own? These stooges cannot solicit an explanation to the question that why Iran does not let Hazara children, born in Iran, attend school? Can these puppets explain why there are no Hazaras doctors or engineers in Iran? They shamelessly neglect the fact that Iran's Islamic Revolutionary Guard Corps (IRGC) is pressing the starving "Barbaris", and hungers stricken "Afghan Donkeys" to fight for them in Syria and Iraq. This current batch of stooges are following footprints of their earlier nonsensical leader who had proclaimed in 1985, "I will turn Quetta into Lebanon." Today, the leaders of the Quds rally are the ones who are leaving no stone unturned in the pursuit of their unaccomplished task of making Quetta another Lebanon.

The bombing of 2010 is a recent one;[1] we should not need history archives to analyse it. Every year, on this nasty day, grief and sadness in the eyes of the community members in Hazara Town and Alamdar Road and the sobbing of the mothers and sisters from the gloomy atmosphere of *"Behesht-e Zainab"*[2] tell us what bereaved families have been going through. In this incident, more than 100 youngsters were murdered[3] and the majority of them were lured to join the protest immediately after Friday prayers. Isn't it ironic that the suicide bomber from the Lashkar-e-Jhangvi (LeJ) who blew himself was keen to go to paradise, and involuntary martyrs were also those tempted by prospects of paradise? What is even more shameful is that the pro-Iran rally leaders still take pride in these 'enforced martyrdoms' instead of offering an honest apology to the bereaved families.

Today, once more, our pro-Iran clerics are planning to sacrifice naive Hazara youngsters to

---

[1] DAWN News, "Suicide bomber strikes Al Quds rally; at least 56 killed", September 04, 2010,
https://www.dawn.com/news/560121/suicide-bomber-strikes-al-quds-rally-at-least-56-killed.

[2] Another name for the Hazara graveyard as glorified by the religious groups

[3] CNN News, "Death toll from Pakistan suicide bombing rises to 73", CNN News, September 04, 2010,
https://edition.cnn.com/2010/WORLD/asiapcf/09/03/pakistan.violence/index.html.

appease Iran and to express solidarity with Mahmoud Abbas and Hamas who, in turn, are determined to create a Salafi state. Once again, they are busy exploiting innocent youth in return for the personal favours they get from Iran. Meanwhile, Iran refuses to offer us anything but hatred, insult, sectarianism, and more deaths. I cannot comprehend how it has impacted Israel and how this has helped the cause of Palestinian liberation after we have been conducting Quds rallies for decades and have sacrificed hundreds of youths in the streets of Quetta in the process. Only an oppressive Israeli soldier or an oppressed Palestinian Muslim brother can tell us how we have impacted the situation with our rallies? All I know is that if we close our eyes and walk blindly in the darkness, our massacre will continue in the name of religion; and the gloomy atmosphere at *Behesht-e Zainab* will remain fraught with sobs and groans of our mothers and sisters.

> *Tarsam narasi ba Ka'aba, Aye A'rabi!*
> *En rah ke Tu merawi ba Turkistan ast*

> O' A'rabi! Thus, you may not get to Ka'aba
> The way you are heading ends in Turkistan

July 22, 2014

---

[18]Hasan Riza Changezi, " عراق اور شام: تباہی کے دہانے پر ", Dawn News, June 19, 2014, https://www.dawnnews.tv/news/1006023.

24

Naya Pakistan and Its Revolutionary Cabinet

After the successful revolution, Prime Minister Imran Khan is presiding over the first cabinet meeting of the revolutionary government. The Captain is seated in the presidential chair in full uniform, pads tied on to his legs, his hands in gloves, and helmet over his head. A cricket bat is lying over the table while he is fidgeting and scuffling a cricket ball in his hands and watching his cabinet with a charismatic smile on his face. Interior minister Attaullah Essa Khelvi is holding his harmonium and sitting to the right of the Prime Minister. From time to time, he closes his eyes and starts humming and his fingers habitually play the harmonium. It sounds like he is working on his next song. To his right, law minister Afzal is seated who once was additional secretary of the election commission. He is holding a small mirror and a small comb in order to discipline his beard. Information minister, Mubashir Luqman, is also seated there with a bundle of files stamped as "most confidential" placed before him. Minister for culture, Sheikh Rashid in his decorative *dhoti*[1] is sitting thereby Mubashir Luqman. A huge piece of phylactery is hanging around his neck and he is habitually curling his macho moustache while staring at his poleaxe.

Minister for religious affairs, Junaid Jamshaid, is also present in his fashionable branded *sherwani*.[2] He has a rosary in his hands which he is praying with a rhythm. Chaudhary Shujaat Hussain, the special assistant to Prime Minister, is sitting to the left of the latter. Captain has assigned him the role of special spokesperson because of his vast experience in clear and articulate communications. He will maintain a status equal to that of a senior federal minister. Foreign minister, Shah Mehmood Qureshi, is seated to the left of Chaudhary Saheb. He is having a mobile phone in his hand and is whispering in English with someone over the phone. Based on his changing facial expressions and the way he is waving his hands; one can assume he is talking about drone attacks. Finance minister, Salman Ahmed, is sitting right next to him in his colourful Sufi cap. A dedicated modernist Sufi, he is wearing a rosary of colourful sacred stone pieces around his neck, and he is frequently tuning his guitar. Minister for overseas Pakistanis and the minister for production, Jehangir Tareen, is having a chat while Javed Miandad, sports minister is having a nap. Shireen Mazari is holding the defence portfolio and sitting at some distance from the

---

[1] Part of the traditional Punjabi rural attire for the lower part of the body

[2] Sherwani is a long coat-like garment worn in the Pakistan and India, also part of Pakistan's national dress

Prime Minister. She is holding a stick in her arm and is unusually silent. Parvez Khattak has been appointed as the minister for science and technology and apparently scrambling about a new mobile phone application. Shehzad Roy is also part of the Captain's cabinet. He will take care of women affairs but at present, he is busy organizing his concerts abroad.

The visionary Captain clears his throat and suddenly all of them go silent with full attention to the leader who starts thus:

"Dear Friends, first of all, I congratulate all of you for establishing the much-awaited *Naya Pakistan*. It is great that we won our first match after long innings. We have to be ready for the next matches as this is the start of our net practice. All of you need to remember that we have to save our wickets and show the world how great batsmen survive a bad pitch. The opponents will attack us with their spin and fast bowlers. They will challenge us with their googlies or ball-tampering, but we have to keep hitting sixes and fours. Remember we are not here to play domestic cricket, but we shall prepare for the world cup. And I do warn, poor performers will not be spared".

After the inspirational presidential address, the Captain pauses for a few moments, and then the striking voice of the interior minister brightens the hearts, "Ae thewa mundari da thewa, sari umar karaan mein teri sewa (O lord I shall serve you all my life)". This triggers finance minister, Sufi Salman Ahmad to take his guitar and Pervez Khattak, minister for science and

---

[3] A special type of dance performed by a troupe of 50 to 100 dancers

information technology, rises in ecstasy and starts dancing *athan*.[3] Before all the revolutionaries lose themselves to a higher state of being, a brief but loud speech disruptively falls on the ears "O Pakistani brothers, for God's sake! Our film industry is on the brink of bankruptcy, Musarrat Shaheen is fed up with movies and starting a career in politics. Where is Najma? Nobody knows. Nargis is not picking her phone. Meera is out of touch while Laila is posing attitude. Has anyone given a damn thought about it?" This was Sheikh Rashid's voice who is standing up holding his poleax. Before he could say more, Mubashir Luqman intercepted him, "I think we all should focus on the media. We should immediately ban anti-state channels." He is not finished. Waving a paper, he has more to say but then the Captain intervenes, "Mubashir, I understand that. Don't worry. We have to clear a lot of mess but before that let me complete my team. I wish to extend this cabinet so that we have idealogues representing every segment of the society. It should look like a national team by all means. Therefore, I have decided to nominate Tahir Ashrafi for the food portfolio and Maulana Fazlur Rehman will be given the ministry of petroleum. I have also decided to assign responsibilities to Abrar ul Haq and Shahid Afridi. As far as provincial governments are concerned, I have talked to local clubs there and I hope that I shall succeed in making good teams there too." With these words, the visionary and charismatic Captain concludes the meeting and prepares to leave as he has

---

[3] A special type of dance performed by a troupe of 50 to 100 dancers

158

to change his dress and wear sherwani for the meeting with the President of Pakistan, Allama Dr. Tahir ul Qadri.

August 27, 2014

Note: This is a piece of satire, written four years before Imran Khan actually was elected Prime Minister of the Islamic Republic of Pakistan.

25

Operation Zarb-e-Azb and Uncle Abdul

ncle Abdul is one of my neighbours. He had high hopes when operation Zarb-e-Azb was launched. In 2013, his son was killed in the twin bombing on Alamdar Road along with hundreds of others.[1] Uncle Abdul was really unfortunate, more so than other parents who had lost their sons, because he could not even hold his son's body in his miserable hands for burial. In the disguise of an ambulance, a vehicle packed with explosives had rammed into the crowd of rescuers and first-responders who were there to help the injured in the first explosion that had occurred tens of minutes ago. The powerful car explosion had simply torn his son's body into unidentifiable countless pieces of meat and ruptured bones. Poor Uncle Abdul, therefore, had posted his son's picture over an empty grave where he would go to mourn the death of his son. His eyes had

---

[1] BBC News, "Pakistan blasts: Shia refuse to bury Quetta bomb dead", BBC News, January 11, 2013,

run out of tears for he used to cry so much but his curious brain had a mountain of complaints and queries.

He used to ask everybody "Can nobody stop these terrorists who have devastated thousands of families?" Whenever I saw him, he would ask the same question to which nobody had any answer. Then Pakistan armed forces launched operation *Zarb-e-Azb* in North Waziristan against the terrorists in June 2014.[2] Uncle Abdul, like most people, seemed relieved for the first time in a while. A minority of people opposed the operation *Zarb-e-Azab* for they were afraid that if the terrorist stronghold was attacked, the terrorists would spread into the entire country, and it would turn into a bigger catastrophe. But Uncle Abdul passionately supported the idea. For him it was already late, but he welcomed the government decision to eliminate terrorists who were responsible for killing fifty thousand people. For the last couple of decades, these Jihadis had established control over tribal areas, and they had been fanning terrorism in the entire region including Pakistan. When operation *Zarb-e-Azb* was eventually launched, religious groups sympathetic to the Taliban, aggressively campaigned to argue that the operation would only worsen the security situation. It was a rather weak argument since Balochistan, especially Quetta, had already been in blood bath for quite some time. The Hazara community had been

---

[2]The Economic Times, "490 Pakistan soldiers, 3,500 militants killed in operation Zarb-e-Azb", The Economic Times, June 15, 2016,

https://economictimes.indiatimes.com/news/defence/490-pakistan-soldiers-3500-militants-killed-in-operation-zarb-e-azb/articleshow/52766005.cms.

targeted in the name of sectarianism for many years. Mutilated bodies of Baloch youngsters were being recovered from desolate places as a routine. All that law enforcement agencies were doing to protect vulnerable communities was building walls around minority communities which would further segregate and marginalize them. Institutions of higher education had already become inaccessible to Hazara students who were frequently attacked. Traders and businessmen from the community were also ambushed. Community members could not perform their religious rituals as the mass slaughter of Hazara women and children continued.

In stark contrast, anti-Shia terrorists and their patronizing political parties audaciously drove into the city in their jeeps with tinted windows and no registration plates. Moreover, armed masked men rallied around the city with impunity and openly chanted hate slogans *"Kafir Kafir Shia Kafir"* in large gatherings. On 14th of March, one such gathering was held at the Hockey ground,[3] right in the heart of the most sensitive security zone where the provincial secretariat, the chief minister's residence, and the governor's house are located literally at stone's throw. Political patrons of the outlawed terrorist organization, Lashkar-e-Jhangvi (LeJ), who had travelled all the way from the Punjab, categorically celebrated 'scoring double centuries' the previous year in Quetta (they amusingly hinted at the bombings in January and February 2013, each of which had killed

[3]DAWN News, "ASWJ supports Taliban talks", DAWN News, March 15, 2014, Https://www.dawn.com/news/1093316.

more than a hundred people including women and children in Hazara Town as well as Alamdar road). All this happened right under the nose of the highest provincial authorities, but provincial government and state agencies didn't even bother questioning them. Instead, they provided them with the protocol and therefore, Ahl-e Sunnat wal Jamaat (ASWJ), the political wing of the Lashkar-e Jhangvi (LeJ) even thanked the provincial government for its hospitality. These appalling developments prompted the Human Rights Watch (HRW) to issue a report under the title of "We are walking dead" in which it addressed the provincial government and state agencies stating, "They should understand that Lashkar-e-Jhangvi should be brought to justice for the massacre they have done. Non action against killings of Hazara and other Shiites is not only indifference and sheer injustice to its citizenry, but it also would mean becoming a party to these crimes".[5]

BBC Urdu noticed some statements in the HRW report which were given by the former commanders of the Frontier Corp (FC) who, on the condition of anonymity, had shared that they saw Hazara community as untrustworthy and agents of Iran.[6]

---

[4]Human Rights Watch, "We are the Walking Dead", Human Rights Watch, June 29, 2014,

Https://www.hrw.org/report/2014/06/29/we-are-walking-dead/killings-shia-hazara-balochistan-pakistan.

[5]IBID

[6]BBC Urdu, "لشکر جھنگوی کے خلاف کارروائی کے علاوہ کوئی چارہ نہیں", BBC Urdu, June 30, 2014,

Https://www.bbc.com/urdu/pakistan/2014/06/140629_human_rights_watch_shia_hazara_rh?fbclid=IwAR0kGxk9P30tDvQrNrVi7ek8PANu6Qm6FgSKa_AV6bM8KEYj9kwj2dAr-Zo.

These anonymous personnel had also said that the Hazaras had exaggerated their persecution so they could seek refuge in any other country and that receive political support and economic aid from Iran.[7] These horrible statements from top commanders of a critical state institution tells a lot about the hate and prejudice against the minority Hazaras. These must be the coldblooded officers in their powerful offices who indifferently watched on as Hazara men, women, and children were being massacred. They never went after the murderers.

And therefore, the *Zarb-e-Azb* offensive came as a fresh breeze of air to people like Uncle Abdul. The operation continued and we would hear the tales of many terrorists shaving their beards to change their outlook and run away from the area. These were the very same people who had imposed a ban on shaving and trimming beards. Uncle Abdul was relieved to hear that the murderers of innocent children and women were desperately running for shelter. He thought that no more parents would have to spend the rest of their lives crying on the empty graves of their beloved children. But his hopes were crushed. When I saw him on Eid day, his face carried the burden of the same old anguish. He just couldn't contain himself and burst open, "Nothing will change. We will continue to be murdered and the governments will continue to watch on indifferently."

I consoled him, "The situation has changed. Don't you think that the law-and-order situation has improved since operation Zarb-e-Azb? Take the

[7] IBI

164

Islamabad dharna for example. The crowd has continued their sit-in for a month and a half already and not a single incident of terrorism has occurred so far. There are many who believe that Imran Khan and Tahir-ul-Qadri are simultaneously Iranian, Israeli, and American agents. Ahl-e Sunnat wal Jamaat (ASWJ) had even taken out a rally in favour of the government and against the sit-in. There were, of course, some hate slogans of "Kafir Kafir" but at least no act of terrorism happened. It means Pakistan is changing for good and that the terrorists are on the run."

Uncle Abdul took a deep breath and protested, "I don't get it. If Pakistan is changing then why can't we spot this change in Balochistan? Is the situation in Balochistan any better than that of North Waziristan? Here too, people are slaughtered in broad daylight, girls' schools are set on fire, acid is thrown on women, dead bodies of youth are recovered from desolate places, bomb explosions are a routine and places of worship are attacked. If government can save Islamabad and the Punjab from terrorism, why can't they save us too? Just on previous Eid, two young boys of my son's age were brutally killed.[8] Their dead bodies were lying on the ground for hours and people walked around indifferently. And what happened on this Eid? Another suicide attacks. Six more people were killed.[9] Aah poor old vegetable vendors, the unfortunate

---

[8] Shehzad Baloch, "Sectarian violence: Two Hazara men shot dead in Quetta", The Express TRIBUNE, August 01, 2014,
https://tribune.com.pk/story/742850/sectarian-violence-two-hazara-men-shot-dead-in-quetta.\

[9] Syed Ali Shah, "Suicide bomber kills five in Quetta's Hazara Town: Police", DAWN News, October 04, 2014, https://www.dawn.com/news/1136201.

woman and three innocent children. How can I believe that operation Zarb-e-Azb will bring peace in Balochistan? How can I believe that our genocide shall freeze, and we shall be able to lead peaceful lives"?

How could I answer Uncle Abdul's questions when I was overwhelmed with many questions myself and my mind was preoccupied with the latest headings in the newspapers: two women attacked with acid in Mastung[10] unidentified gunmen killed two men from Hazara community[11] six women seriously hurt from an acid attack in Pishin[12] the attack on the Zikri Baloch community Eight people reported dead[13] a girls' school set on fire in Kech[14] Daesh's presence cannot be ruled

[10]Syed Ali Shah, "Two women wounded in Mastung acid attack", DAWN News, July 23, 2014,

https://www.dawn.com/news/1120871/two-women-wounded-in-mastung-acid-attack

[11]Shehzad Baloch, "Sectarian violence: Two Hazara men shot dead in Quetta", The Express TRIBUNE, August 01, 2014,

https://tribune.com.pk/story/742850/sectarian-violence-two-hazara-men-shot-dead-in-quetta.

[12]The Nation, "Six women injured in Pishin acid attack", The Nation, August 01, 2014,

https://nation.com.pk/01-Aug-2014/six-women-injured-in-pishin-acid-attack.

[13]Aljazeera News, "Gunmen target minority sect in Pakistan", Aljazeera News, August 29, 2014,

https://www.aljazeera.com/news/2014/08/29/gunmen-target-minority-sect-in-pakistan/.

[14]DAWN News, "School set on fire in Kech district", DAWN News, September 03, 2014,

https://www.dawn.com/news/1129567.

[15]Syed Ali Shah, "Cannot rule out the presence of IS militants in Balochistan", DAWN News, October 08, 2014,

https://www.dawn.com/news/1136638.

out (Chief Minister, Dr Abdul Malik Malik)[15] sectarian terrorists are provided safe havens in Balochistan (Human Rights Commission of Pakistan)[16] three million people forced to displace within Balochistan (HRCP).[17]

The original article was first published on DAWN Urdu website on October 21, 2014. [18]

[16]BBC Urdu, " بلوچستان میں مذہبی گروہوں کے لیے جگہ بنائی جا رہی ہے ", BBC Urdu, October 12, 2014, https://www.bbc.com/urdu/multimedia/2014/10/141012_balochistan_ext remism_hrreport_nj?ocid=socialflow_twitter.

[17]DAWN News, "Flight from Balochistan", DAWN News, October 14, 2014, https://www.dawn.com/news/1137770.

[18]Hassan Riza Changezi, " آپریشن ضرب عضب اور چاعبدل ", DAWN Urdu, October 21, 2014.

26

Room for Improvement

In 1977, when general Zia-ul-Haq deposed Prime Minister Zulfiqar Ali Bhutto and imposed martial law, I was a student of 6th grade. The self-proclaimed commander of the faithful, Zia-ul-Haq, assumed the charge of Chief Martial Law Administrator as well as Patron in Chief of Pakistan Boys Scouts Association. I was a member of Pakistan Boys Scouts Association and owing to my participation in a school ceremony, I got an opportunity to shake hands with the commander of the faithful. Perhaps, therefore, I have maintained interest in his politics and character. The famous catchphrase "By the Grace of Allah" was introduced by General Zia-ul-Haq which his disciples repeat with devotion to this day. His legacy includes a number of proverbs and ideological slogans, one of which I still remember, and which has left an indelible impact on Pakistani state and society. He would proudly state, "First we are Muslims, and then Pakistanis."

You may disagree but I believe these holy words spelled out of the holy mouth of the commander of the faithful, transformed the very meaning of Pakistani nationality. Although there was always the dearth of a binding concept of unity and solidarity which can define a collective of people and groups from various regions as one nation but somehow people, with a varying degree of political association, saw themselves as 'Pakistanis.' Balochistan and Sindh provinces always had reservations and complaints from the big brother, the Punjab, but despite all these differences people still felt politically committed to 'Pakistan.' Particularly, followers of various faiths and religions did not hesitate to subscribe to the idea of Pakistan, and this was, perhaps, the factor that brought Pakistanis together and produced the sense of sharing one modern national identity.

This golden slogan from the Amir-ul-Momineen (Commander of the Faithful, General Zia-ul-Haq) immediately assigned second class citizenship to Pakistanis of other faiths. Within Pakistan's Muslims, this created a toxic debate of competing identities: are they Sunni or Shia first and Pakistanis next? I would complain less, had this toxicity been contained at that level. Soon, this created a flurry of sectarian debates and competing political identities of Deobandi, Barelvi, and the Ahl-e Hadith. This created a cycle of sectarian division where every sect was pitched against the others to compete and ensure their version of Islam and Sharia get to be recognized and adopted by the state. Then, violent political groups mushroomed across the country who would call out each other openly and jeopardized the very fabric of the state and society. On the other hand, racial discrimination was also hatched so that people from different classes entangle themselves into fight and turn their attention away from the basic issues of country. Therefore, factions were encouraged to do anything extra judicial in a bid to silence opponents of the martial law government. In the same way, racial, tribal, criminal and armed groups were introduced in Balochistan to fan the flames of hatred and violence.

During Zia ul Haq's rule, the intelligence agencies and other institutions were persuaded towards extremism in order to produce Jihadi Culture to achieve America's objectives. The impact of his policy was too deep that even succeeding governments could not dare to modify it, even the Pakistan People's Party that claims to be the champion of public rights and being secular not only pursued Zia-ul-Haq's policy but even took part in the formation of Taliban in a bid to make Afghanistan at least subservient to Pakistan if not the fifth province of Pakistan.

What happened after that or what is happening, we do not need to go into details but suffice it to say that we are paying the price. Although it may be futile to blame oneself for the self-inflicted wound, it is also a fact that mistakes can be rectified only if one accepts their flaws or at least have a sense of what they have done. According to media reports, during the last 15 years, more than fifty thousand Pakistanis have died of terrorist attacks; aside from ordinary people a large portion of the victims are from law enforcement institutions including some high-ranking members.

During this period, they have tried to target most sensitive zones of Pakistan which is an indication of their hell-bent determination. Perhaps this is the reason that after years, the tone of the ruling class, particularly the armed forces of Pakistan has changed, and it can be assessed from December 2012 doctrine. Express Tribune published a detailed analysis in this regard on January 2, 2013 stating that the Armed forces of Pakistan has declared militancy as a threat to national sovereignty.[1]

It was mentioned in the report that Pakistan always thought India as its top enemy but growing militancy has forced Pakistan to reconsider its strategy.[2] Operation *Zarb-e-Azb* launched in June 2013 should be seen in that perspective when after months of preparation, the military launched well planned targeted attacks on terrorists' safe havens in North Waziristan.[3] In fact, the Nawaz government was on the horns of a dilemma till the very end of the operation. According to reports, more than a thousand foreign and domestic terrorists have been killed whereas a major part of South Waziristan has been cleared from the grip of terrorists which is surely very encouraging.[4]

---

[1]The Express TRIBUNE, "New doctrine: Army identifies 'homegrown militancy' as biggest threat", The Express TRIBUNE, January 02, 2013,

https://tribune.com.pk/story/488362/new-doctrine-army-identifies-homegrown-militancy-as-biggest-threat.

[2]IBID

[3]The Express TRIBUNE, "Operation Zar-e-Azb: Airstrikes leave 15 militants dead in Khyber Agency", The Express TRIBUNE, October 04, 2014,

https://tribune.com.pk/story/771181/operation-zarb-e-azb-airstrikes-leave-15-militants-dead-in-khyber-agency.

With the fast-changing world around us, we need to deal with our internal affairs with utmost seriousness. We would be living in fool's paradise if we believed that Pakistan would be safe from the emerging threats of ISIS. There is widespread news that a large number of Pakistani militants have also joined the ranks of ISIS. Balochistan's Chief Minister Dr. Malik Baloch's interview is on the record wherein he had said that the presence of ISIS or Daesh cannot be ruled out in Balochistan.[5] He also spoke to BBC in September 2013 that militants from Balochistan are going to Syria to join the war. There are also reports that there is a growing ISIS footprint in Balochistan. Meanwhile, many Taliban commanders have also joined ISIS. Although Pakistan has denied the news, yet there is a great concern that if Pakistan does not tackle the problem with earnestness, it could face serious problems in the future. We ought to remember that the prevailing chaos and unrest in Pakistan is caused by the very same militants who were once under our compassionate tutelage. But when they returned, they ran us over. Here, the question arises: do the government and state institutions realize the fact that once these extremists come back from the Middle East, they wouldn't pose a big threat to the sovereignty of

[4]The Economic Times, "490 Pakistan soldiers, 3,500 militants killed in operation Zar-e-Azb", The Economic Times, January 15, 2016, https://economictimes.indiatimes.com/news/defence/490-pakistan-soldiers-3500-militants-killed-in-operation-zarb-e-azb/articleshow/52766005.cms.

[5]Syed Ali Shah, "Cannot rule out the presence of IS militants in Balochistan: Dr Malik", DAWN News, October 08, 2014,

https://www.dawn.com/news/1136638.

our country?

Let's leave aside its role in politics in the past, there is no denying the fact that Pakistani army is considered one of the best armies in the world. Although the armed forces often come under criticism for improper interference in civilian affairs or toppling of the elected governments, and there is a possibility of disagreement with their policies but despite all the criticism, it is a fact that the Pakistani army is an organized and strong institution which has the capability to combat terrorism. We already have witnessed their capability in Swat and Malakand divisions. This is high time for the government and the armed forces to design a comprehensive strategy in order to get rid of the domestic terrorists. There is room for improvement only if we accept all our previous mistakes and ought to focus on our own problems rather than interfere in the affairs of our neighbouring countries.

The original article was published on DAWN Urdu website on October 30, 2014.

27

If Daesh Settles in . . .

There is a notable consternation within the social and political circles of Balochistan since the top-secret letter of Balochistan's interior minister leaked out on the potential activities of the international terrorist organization of the Islamic State (ISIS) or Daesh, particularly its linkages with Pakistan's local terrorist organizations of Lashkar-e-Jhangvi (LeJ) and the Ahle Sunnat wal Jamaat (ASWJ). According to newspapers, this letter was issued on October 21, and it warned the concerned authorities about the potential wave of fresh attacks.[1] Although the chief minister, Abdul Malik Baloch, had previously been positive about a possible presence of the deadly ISIS in the province but lately, he has changed his stance and has declined it.[2] Despite the

---

[1]Mubashir Zaidi, "داعش کی پاکستان میں ہزاروں افراد کی بھرتی کا انکشاف", DAWN (Urdu), November 08, 2014, https://www.dawnnews.tv/news/1012059.

[2]Syed Ali Shah, "بلوچستان میں داعش موجود نہیں، وزیراعلیٰ", DAWN (Urdu), October 26, 2014, https://www.dawnnews.tv/news/1011467.

pro-ISIS graffiti which have appeared on the walls
across multiple cities in Pakistan,[3] federal interior
minister, Chaudhary Nisar, continues to reject any
possibility of the presence of ISIS or Daesh in Pakistan.
While the government has persisted in its denial of ISIS
on the Pakistani soil, a statement was issued by the
banned organization of Jundullah which confirmed a
meeting between their leaders and a delegation from
ISIS.[4]

The debate on whether ISIS has found a foothold
in Pakistan is far from over. In the meanwhile, there are
increasing reports of pro-ISIS graffiti and
dissemination of pamphlets across the country from
Karachi in the south to Gilgit in the north. Although the
Director-General of Inter-Services Public Relations
(ISPR), Major General Asim Bajwa, has repeatedly said
that ISIS will have no room in Pakistan,[5] his statement
has failed to quash the valid concerns many Pakistanis
have. And hence, the Chief of Army Staff of Pakistan,
General Raheel Sharif, in his recent visit to the United
States, had to reaffirm his commitment not to allow
ISIS any space in Afghanistan and Pakistan.

Federal interior minister, Chaudhary Nisar, said
that ISIS or Daesh was an Arab organization and that it
had nothing to do with Pakistan.[6] It would be pertinent

[3]DAWN Urdu Desk, " پاکستان میں داعش کی موجودگی کا امکان مسترد ", DAWN (Urdu), November 11,
2014, https://www.dawnnews.tv/news/1012182.

[4]AP, " داعش، جنداللہ کی بلوچستان میں ملاقات ", DAWN (Urdu), November 12, 2014,
https://www.dawnnews.tv/news/1012249/.

[5]DAWN, " پاکستان میں داعش کوئی خطرہ نہیں، فوج ", DAWN (Urdu), November 16, 2014,
https://www.dawnnews.tv/news/1012401.

[6]DAWN Urdu Desk, " داعش عرب تنظیم ہے، پاکستان سے تعلق نہیں، وزیر داخلہ ", DAWN (Urdu),
November 22, 2014, https://www.dawnnews.tv/news/1012684.

to remind Chaudhary of the fact that Al-Qaida remains an Arab organization too and that not only it terrorized Pakistan but also produced a whole generation of Arab and non-Arab Jihadis. These official denials are not convincing enough because there is a history to them. Chaudhary Nisar needs to be reminded that Pakistan always denied Usama bin Laden's presence on Pakistani soil but eventually, he was busted right under our nose in Abbottabad, close to the army garrison. Recently, a story in Dawn claimed that ISIS had nominated a former Afghan Jihadi Commander, Muslim Dost, as the Amir (Head) of Khurasan Belt.[7] India, Bangladesh, Afghanistan and Central Asian states and several other countries fall under this belt. For a moment, this sounded like a joke. It seemed as if we had stepped back in time and as if a king was arbitrarily distributing properties among his favourites. But then hearing the news of Daesh dedicated to introducing their own standard coins of gold and silver[8] which could actually become the most precious currency of the world, I realized we better take this seriously.

Remember that Daesh has already captured major cities of Syria and Iraq which are rich in oil. In addition, seizure of the banks in those regions have turned ISIS into the richest terrorist organization

7Zahir Shah Sherazi, "ابراہیم مسلم دوست داعش کے خراسان کے امیر مقرر", DAWN (Urdu), November 13, 2014,

https://www.dawnnews.tv/news/1012319.

8DAWN Urdu Desk, "داعش کا سونے چاندی کی کرنسی متعارف کرانے کا فیصلہ", DAWN (Urdu), November 11, 2014,

https://www.dawnnews.tv/news/1012202.

internationally.[9] With that amount of wealth at their disposal, it should not be difficult for the organization to attract mercenary jihadis from around the world. There are also reports of former Saddam commanders training new ISIS recruits on how to fly captured airplanes.[10] Even if there is little evidence that ISIS could manage an aerial force, this indicates how ambitious the deadly terrorist organization is. Given the large-scale violence that ISIS has unleashed in large parts of Iraq and Syria, it is only natural that any possibility of ISIS emergence in this region will scare the hell out of citizens of Balochistan. There have been too many false claims by the government in recent years and the region has seen a lot of violence and devastation.

Therefore, it is an easy job for ISIS to recruit mercenaries. There are also reports that former pilots are training ISIS mercenaries. The people of Pakistan particularly, people in Balochistan are concerned about the rapid growth of ISIS and the non-serious attitude of the government.

According to statistics, over 1500 civilians have fallen prey to sectarian terrorism in Balochistan and most of them belong to the Hazara Community. In a parallel thread, Baloch nationalists claim that over

[9]Amanda Macias, Jeremy Bender, "Here's How the World's Richest Terrorist Group Makes Millions Everyday", Business Insider, August 28, 2014,

https://www.businessinsider.com/isis-worlds-richest-terrorist-group-2014-8.

[10]DAWN Urdu Desk, "داعش جنگجوؤں کو جہاز اڑانے کی تربیت دینے کے", DAWN (Urdu), October 17, 2014,

https://www.dawnnews.tv/news/1011064.

2000 Baloch men have been killed in the last fifteen years. Hazara community has made persistent demands for the arrest of the culprits involved in such heinous crimes, but serious efforts are yet to be witnessed in this regard by law enforcement agencies. Some Baloch nationalists also think that sectarian terrorism is deliberately spread into the province in order to declare Baloch nationalists responsible for it and pave the way for an operation against Baloch nationalists.

Sectarian Terrorism started in 1999 in Balochistan and the Baloch separatist movement in 2003. One cannot deny the fact that sectarian violence also amplified since the separatist movement engulfed Balochistan. The state's response has been different to the sectarian and the separatist movements. Baloch nationalists have been killed, and their mutilated bodies thrown into desolated places[11] while the sectarian terrorists are set free from jails.[12,13] This is the main reason why people cast doubt at the role of the law enforcement agencies. Some hard-line analysts in Balochistan think that if sectarian terrorism was

---

[11]Zahid Gishkori, "Around 1000 bodies recovered from Balochistan in six years", The News International, July 25, 2016,
https://www.thenews.com.pk/print/137462-Around-1000-bodies-recovered-from-Balochistan-in-six-years.

[12]The News International, "Usman Kurd, the man who caused fall of Raisani govt", The News International, January 15, 2013,
https://www.thenews.com.pk/archive/print/627907-usman-kurd,-the-man-who-caused-fall-of-raisani-govt.

[13]AFP, "Extremist leader Malik Ishaq set free from jail", DAWN, September 11, 2012, https://www.dawn.com/news/748652/malik-ishaq-released-from-prison.

[14]Muhammad Kazim, "کوئٹہ میں بس پر فائرنگ سے آٹھ شیعہ ہزارہ ہلاک", BBC Urdu, October 23, 2014,
https://www.bbc.com/urdu/pakistan/2014/10/141023_hazara_killed_in_quetta_zz.

eliminated and peace prevailed in the province, then the services of the Frontier Corps (FC) would no longer be needed. At this moment, FC, a federal law enforcing agency is getting paid for their services by the provincial government of Balochistan. Remember that on October 23, nine Hazara fruit vendors were killed in Hazarganji[14] and the next day, Lashkar-e-Jhangvi claimed responsibility for the attack and even threatened to carry out more attacks in the future. The public was furious with the unsatisfactory government response. Where is the government? How is it possible that a non-state extremist organization can hijack the whole society and issue threats with full impunity?

I believe that the situation in Pakistan is not as bad as in Iraq or Syria. Afterall, this is the world's fifth powerful country with nuclear technology. And yet, Pakistan is the world's third most affected country from terrorism. [15]

It worries me to death to imagine if Daesh or sectarian terrorists are not uprooted from the country, how would Pakistan survive? Will Pakistan continue foreign relations under these defunct organizations? Shall the nuclear assets of Pakistan be safe from the hands of terrorists? These are the most fundamental questions worth considering.

December 08, 2014

---

[15]DAWN Urdu Desk, " پاکستان دہشت گردی سے متاثر، تیسرا بڑا ملک ", DAWN (Urdu), November 08, 2014,
https://www.dawnnews.tv/news/1012496.

28

Terrorism - Factors, Effects and Remedies

What is terrorism? There is no scientific or a universal definition for it. In today's day and age, there are some variations in it in accordance with the ideology one associates it with. In my opinion, terrorism is an act of an individual, a group, an institution or a government imposing their ideology, belief, policy or desire by means of violence and threats with little or no regard to people's basic human rights.

If we intend to cover its history and background, books after books would be required. In short, it would be sufficient to say that the history of terrorism is as old as mankind. Terrorism can be justified by many as an ideology. Jihad in the name of expanding one's belief, wars backed by fascist motivations, revolutions to impose new ideologies and violence, rapes, massacres, mass killings, looting, building towers consisting of human skulls, and power quests are all acts of terrorism. Meanwhile, some factions might term their acts of beheadings or hanging their opponents to death as Jihad while their opponents would definitely call these acts as terrorism.

In recent history, millions of people were killed during the first and second world wars. Also, decades long cold war affected the whole world and resulted in the spread of terrorism. Apparently, the cold war has ended but many countries are still on fire as a result of ongoing tussles among world powers. Our region has been suffering from terrorism for the past four decades. There can be multiple factors behind terrorism but as far as I can think of, there are global and regional actors active behind terrorism in our region which are trying to impose a policy of their choice. I believe revolutions and rebellions of the 1970s (whatever you name them) were direct consequences of the hegemonic struggle between Soviet Union, the champion of socialism and the United States of America, the champion of capitalism. This tug of war pushed the whole region into a downward spiral of violence and destruction that still haunt millions of people in this region. Around the same period, the changes in Pakistan, Afghanistan, and Iran note the order in which they rolled out with little time delays were all brought by the policy choices of the superpowers. Millions of people lost their lives and millions others were uprooted from their home and lands just to seek refuge in other countries. A whole generation of humans in this region lost their education and better economic opportunities. They were later used as fuel in the following decades of proxy wars.

It is an open secret now that the United States trained and armed thousands of jihadis on the Afghan and Pakistani soil in order to overthrow the Soviet-backed People's Democratic Party of Afghanistan (PDPA). With funds from Iran and Arab countries and weapons from the US and Pakistan, the mix of jihadis killed a generation of people. Fanning religious extremism was an integral component of this jihad strategy. Additionally, the Arab-Iran rivalry to influence and lead the Muslim world further accelerated sectarianism. Under the policy slogan that "Islam knows no borders," the Khomeini regime made efforts to export their revolution into Afghanistan, Pakistan and other countries in the Middle East and Central Asia. Undoubtedly, this contributed to fanning the fire of sectarianism which has engulfed the whole region.

It was not just a coincidence that only months after the Iranian revolution, an ambitious Shia organization was established in Pakistan titled, "Tehreek Nifaz-e Fiqh-e Jafaria" (Movement for Imposition of the Jafari (Shia) Jurisprudence.)[1] Not only it demanded imposition of the Shia jurisprudence in Pakistan but also campaigned for an Iran-like revolution. This was precisely the time when Arab jihadis flocked to Pakistan and Afghanistan whose apparent mission was to take part in jihad in Afghanistan. During this period, not only a large

---

[1] Global Security.Org, "Tehrik-Jafria Pakistan (TJP)", Global Security.org, July 09, 2018,
https://www.globalsecurity.org/military/world/para/tjp.htm.

number of religious seminaries mushroomed across Pakistan to train Jihadis under the patronage of Arab countries but also to counter the Iranian influence, anti-Shia scholars were further patronized. And thus, a proxy war began in Pakistan which was fuelled by Iran and Saudi Arabia.

The bloody clashes between Shia activists and the military government of General Zia-ul Haq on July 6, 1985, was the starting point of the sectarian journey which would set Pakistan on fire in the upcoming decades.[2] Only after a couple of months, an anti-Shia group named Anjuman Sipah-e Sahaba (ASS, later becoming Sipah Sahaba Pakistan or SSP), was established in the Jhang city in the Punjab.[3] In the years since, the mayhem and chaos that these two sectarian organizations and their countless offshoots have created in the Punjab, pushed Nawaz brothers to strike agreements with these organizations. The agreement parochially focused on bringing peace to Punjab. After agreements in the late 1990s, Nawaz league bagged several Sunni extremist organizations in their ranks as their political and social allies. Many of these Sunni jihadi organizations established chapters in Balochistan soon afterwards.

These sectarian militants selected the Mastung

[2]Malik Siraj Akbar, "Hazara tribesmen under attack in Quetta", Hazara International, February 06, 2009,

https://www.hazarapeople.com/2009/02/06/hazara-tribesmen-under-attack-in-quetta/.

[3]Mapping Militant Organisations, "Sipah-e-Sahaba Pakistan", Stanford University, February 15, 2012,

https://web.stanford.edu/group/mappingmilitants/cgi-bin/groups/view/147.

district along the RCD (Regional Cooperation and Development) highway as their hub. Adjacent to Quetta, Mastung is strategically an important hub for all trade and traffic between Pakistan and Iran. After establishing themselves, the sectarian organizations cleansed Mastung off of its recent Shia converts. This was a clear message for those who had converted to Shia Islam and who were perceived to be increasing the Iranian influence in this region.

Under the pretext of sectarianism, hundreds of attacks on the Hazaras since are part of the history. Thousands of people from all walks of life have been gunned down. Remember, I am talking about those terrorist organizations who according to media reports receive millions of dollars from Saudi Arabia and other gulf countries. On the other side, there are also media reports about Iranian backing of Pakistani Shia organizations who are involved in the killings of their opponents. As far as the state institutions are concerned, it is not difficult to conclude that peace in the Punjab is their priority and they also want to save these militant organizations for their ambitious strategic projects outside Pakistan. Therefore, they have directed the army of sectarian terrorists to Balochistan; to Hazaras, precisely speaking.

It is worth mentioning here that the accelerated attacks on Hazaras since the murder of Nawab Akbar Bugti in August 2006[4] is also no coincidence. We should

---

[4] Saleem Shahid, "Bugti killed in operation: Six officers among 21 security personnel dead", DAWN News, August 27, 2006,

https://www.dawn.com/news/207726/bugti-killed-in-operation-six-officers-among-21-security-personnel-dead.

keep in mind that the latest wave of the Baloch secessionist movement started in 2003 which gained huge momentum after the murder of Nawab Akbar Bugti in August 2006. This was accompanied by an increase in the number of attacks on the province's settler communities. Strange as it was, the Inspector General of Police once suggested targeted killings were the ultimate remedy to the prevalent ill of target killings. We soon witnessed an increase in cases of abduction and target-killings of Baloch nationalists as well as an increase in terrorist attacks on the Hazara community. To some extent, the powerful establishment succeeded in diverting the international attention away from the ongoing Baloch secessionist question and onto the persecution of the ethnic Hazara community. To set the records straight, let me assert that this is not an accusation. In December 2013, the interior minister Chaudhary Nisar himself announced disarming the 'patriotic and people-friendly' militias who were allegedly created during the former chief minister Nawab Aslam Raisani's tenure.[5] These private militias were involved in terrorism, street crimes and bloodshed on a large scale. According to media reports, the same private groups were not only behind the abduction and killings of Baloch nationalist activists but also the terrorist attacks on the members of the Hazara community.

This, however, raises a question. Since Baloch

---

[5]The Express TRIBUNE, "Security concerns: Nisar maps out Balochistan plan", The Express TRIBUNE, December 30, 2013,

https://tribune.com.pk/story/651764/security-concerns-nisar-maps-out-balochistan-plan.

separatist movement is not just limited to Balochistan in Pakistan but also the parts of Balochistan under Iran, both Pakistan and Iran, sharing a common agenda, are fanning the flames of sectarianism just so they can overshadow the Baloch separatist movements within their respective borders? Would they consider the sacrifice of some peaceful and innocent civilians a bad bargain?

Some analysts believe international powers who are after the vast mineral riches and strategic goals in this region could be behind this wave of terrorism. I question the notion of killing innocent Hazara children, women and men, only to gain access to the rich resources in this region? There are far more natural resources in the middle eastern and central Asian countries. Why are those nations not suffering our fate? In fact, many international powers are doing their best to lure these nations into international trade. By casting doubt on all these alternative explanations, I mean to express that, as I view things, terrorism in Pakistan is heavily related to the regional hegemonic competition between Iran and its Arab rivals and the resulting proxy wars that keep finding theatres of violence in Iraq, Syria, Afghanistan, and Pakistan. To sustain their authoritarian regimes and to increase their influence in this region, they fan sectarianism and keep communities engaged in a state of heightened sectarian politics. This is further aided by the fragile state institutions in Pakistan and persistent negligence of Pakistan's consecutive ruling elites. As a weak state, Pakistan is not only unable to curb foreign influence and intervention in its domestic politics, but it is also compelled to manipulate power groups against one another in order to gain relative advantage as a moderator. State institutions are far from being on the same page and have even worked to secure interests of foreign powers at the cost of increased sectarianism and ruptured social fabric. Opportunism from local land mafia, drug lords and identity-based business rivalry would constitute a third factor that has pushed our society to the unfortunate state where we find ourselves today.

As the current state of affairs stand, citizenry in Quetta remains divided in ethnic and sectarian enclaves, segregated by high walls and heavily guarded check posts. Hazaras have lost their footing in businesses, education and employment. Many thousands have abandoned their properties in Quetta and embarked on dangerous journeys to seek a safer life elsewhere.

How can we counter terrorism? The answer is as difficult as easy the question is. If we believe this terrorism has been imposed upon us in the garb of sectarianism and the main agency lay with foreign powers who have found their local facilitators, then we need to figure out how much can we counter these forces? Can we ignore all our differences and unite? That would be unnatural. Can we convince Saudi Arabia and Iran to please spare us? Can we demand the Baloch activists to forget all injustices and just stay calm? Can we convince the Shia community to convert to Sunni Islam so they can be spared? Can we all collectively emigrate to a new island?

If we cannot do any of the above, then we shall

have to learn to face the challenges and live a life of dignity. We can disagree on many issues, but we have to avoid the constant bickering and instead support each other in the community. We need to learn to respect beliefs and ideologies of others as much as we do our own. If we want increased tolerance in this society, we will have to pioneer. We may not be able to put an end to terrorism against us, but we can raise our voice against this injustice on every available forum. We will have to think out of the box on how to strengthen our relations with our neighbouring communities. We will have to extend our solidarity and empathize with them in their hours of pain and agony. We need to clearly, loudly, and explicitly condemn religious extremism in all its forms, and we will have to resist anyone who wants to direct this society towards more divisions, more intolerance and more hate. I am convinced that we may not be able to uproot terrorism, but we can plant an alternative idea, build a new platform, establish a new network which would ultimately help our younger generations to move towards a society free of terrorism.

This article was read in a community conference organized by the Progressive Academic Forum on October 21, 2014.

29

Extremism and the Youth

believe extremism is a psychological behaviour that forces human beings to forget all about the values of tolerance, harmony, and moderation when it comes to everyday affairs particularly those involving political and religious beliefs. Such individuals not only consider their ideology and beliefs the ultimate truth but also seek to implement them on others that results in anarchy and disruption in the social system. If this psychological condition, also known as extremism and fanaticism, is accompanied by the elements of force and violence, it becomes terrorism. Now the question arises about what moderation is and how to determine the borderline where it transforms into extremism? It is important to ask whether it has the same standard in every society, or there is room for variations?

I think there can be different units to gauge moderation. For instance, we inhabit certain geographical boundaries where state laws determine our limits to help maintain order in society. According to the laws of the state, every individual must have the right to adhere to their beliefs and must enjoy complete freedom to practice their religious rituals. Just as Muslims have the right to practice their religion in mosques and other places of worship, so do the Hindus, Sikhs, and Christians who practice their faith in their temples and churches. They are allowed complete freedom to express their faith in private if they wish to do so. Now if a Muslim, instead of offering his prayers at home or in a mosque, forcefully enters a temple or a church to offer his prayers, he is exceeding his limits. Similarly, if he breaks into neighbouring houses to offer his prayers or insists on praying on the roads and still believes it is his legitimate right, he is then a vivid example of extremism. Likewise, drivers driving on the road should abide by traffic laws. And if they fail to do so, they could end up posing a big threat to other road users as well as face penalty charges. These regulations determine everyone's jurisdictions and help maintains discipline on the road. Violating these laws would result in accidents and chaos on the roads.

Some issues do not fall within the purview of state laws. However, religion and established social norms help to prevent chaos in society. In our state laws, there is no punishment for telling lies that we utter all day long. But perhaps there exists no religion or culture in the world that rewards their followers for this bad deed. So, it can be said that religion and social norms and values determine our jurisdiction in one way or the other and their violations can cause chaos in society.

The leading cause of rampant terrorism and killings in our country is this extremism. There is a famous saying, "Your liberty ends where my nose begins." To put it simply, everyone has the right to live a life according to their wishes, however, they should respect other individuals' rights as much as they takes care of theirs. Everyone has distinct likes and dislikes, so they should have complete freedom to live their life according to their ideology and wishes. Although everyone has the right to deprecate with others' ideology as much as he is committed to his own; but this should not mean imposing your beliefs on others. For instance, when someone tries to impose his ideology on others that would definitely result in terrorism, which we see is prevailing in our contemporary society.

As a repercussion of this extremist ideology, an ordinary Muslim considers it a sin to share a food plate with a Hindu despite the latter being cleaner and observing civility. On the other hand, eating the spit of dirty witchcraft or drinking camel urine which is contaminated with numerous unknown illnesses are considered virtuous deeds and divine blessings. Similarly, in remembrance of the martyrs of Karbala, some Shia Muslims perform *tatbir*[1] causing their blood to flow on the streets because they believe it will bring a religious reward in the afterlife but are reluctant to donate blood to patients in hospitals who are in dire need of it.

The result of extremist thoughts is that if Barelvis mistakenly offer their prayers behind an Imam from

---

[1] A bloodletting ritual practised as an act of mourning by Shia Muslims

the Deobandi sect of Islam, then renewal of their Nikah[2] become compulsory. The adherents of Deobandi denomination of Islam consider it a sin to shake hands with Shias whom they consider infidels. Due to this extremist ideology, ordinary Muslims believe that all the big sins such as rape, murder, theft, and money extortion from orphans and widows would be forgiven by God, if they perform pilgrimage to Hajj and of Imam Reza Shrine. Those who cannot afford to be pilgrims may recite a short verse from the Holy Quran written on board fixed on the main door of *Behesht-e-Zainab*[3]. People are made to believe that all their current and future sins would be exonerated if they recited those verses. Those who believe in this myth persuade others to believe in it as well. And when others choose to disagree with their views, they immediately declare them *Kafirs* (Infidels) without any further research. I wonder who would dare to stop those from committing anti-social and criminal activities, repeatedly telling lies, stealing, strangulating weak people to death, and slaughtering others while chanting Allahu Akbar[4] because they have strong faith that the door to forgiveness is never shut on them?

There is no age limit for becoming an extremist, neither it is restricted to any belief or ideology. A nationalist would be an extremist if he considers his nation superior and looks down upon others and tries to find ways to exploit the weaker nations. A socialist would be an extremist if he declares his opponents as

---

[2] Muslim marriage contract

[3] Another name for Hazara Graveyard

[4] God is great

revisionists and puppets of capitalists and imperialists and considers his views as the ultimate truth. A writer and intellectual would be an extremist if he tags all other views except his as useless, childish, and rubbish and tirelessly persuades others to follow his perspective. In my opinion, there is no difference between an extremist mullah, a nationalist, or a socialist who justifies sacrificing the poor and the weak in the name of revolution, paradise or for some political gains. There is absolutely no doubt that due to lack of tolerance and extremism, this whole region including our country is going through fire and blood. We would only be able to overcome extremism and terrorism when we teach our youth to respect other people's beliefs as much as they respect their own ideology and belief. They could pray day and night, advocate nationalism or communism or do nothing. However, they should mind their boundaries. Youth should be taught not to interfere in other peoples' matters or compel others to follow their paths; because no Hindu is fond of going to Muslim's Paradise to enjoy sexual intercourse with seventy-two virgins.[5] They prefer to go to their own Swarga[6] where most of the Hindu Devatas reside alongside the Hanuman, the monkey god; and where sacred cows are grazing in peace. Therefore, in my humble view, instead of motivating others to our paradise, we should focus on our own deeds. It is my conviction that if we really want our new generation to come out of the prevailing chaotic

---

[5]Voluptuously beautiful young woman in Islamic eschatology

[6]Heaven, specifically the heaven presided over by God Indra, where virtuous souls reside before reincarnation

situation, then we ought to remain moderate, observe mutual respect, avoid imposing our ideology on others, and develop the environment to discuss issues democratically.

Therefore, we must promote the philosophy of mutual respect, tolerance, and peaceful co-existence to turn our society into a living example of a paradise. We need to avoid turning our community into hell for an unseen and utopian paradise.

How this caravan of life is moving on!
Seize the moment that passes with joy!
Oh cupbearer, why worry what rivals will do tomorrow?
Bring the cup before the night passes!

The original article was published on DAWN Urdu website on February 14, 2015.[7]

[7]Hassan Riza Changezi, "ایسا کیوں ہوتا ہے؟", DAWN Urdu, January 30, 2013, Https://www.dawnnews.tv/news/57111/aisa-kyun-hota-hai-riza-changezi-aq.

30

The First Brick

As far as I can recall, the issue of load-shedding in Pakistan dates back to the period of Commander of the Faithful, Gen. Zia-ul-Haq as the President. Those were the cold winter days. I cannot say for certain about the rest of the country but in Quetta, the use of natural gas for domestic purposes was not initiated yet. Back then, people would use electric heaters and coal stoves to keep their houses warm. Therefore, when people were subjected to long hours of load-shedding daily, they were outraged. The government, in an attempt to tackle the problem, issued a statement on a national TV channel. It was explained that due to sub-zero temperatures, the glaciers on top of the mountains had frozen causing a drop in the water level in rivers. This water scarcity, in turn, had caused significant hurdle in the process of generating electricity. To overcome this power shortage, the government had to resort to load-shedding in residential areas to continue the supply of electricity to the industries to keep the wheels of the economy running. This was, by all means, a scientific explanation and, therefore, proved convincing to the educated citizens who silently accepted it as their fate. They expected that the load-shedding would end in a couple of months. They hoped the winter would be over soon and the waters in the rivers would rise again to a level sufficient enough to generate electricity in the country. But their hopes turned into despair when the load-shedding, not only stretched over to June and July but also increased in its durations. But before people would come out to protest, the government issued another statement. This time people were told that as in the summer, the use of air conditioners and fans increases, the shortage of electricity befalls. To overcome this shortage, the government uses load-shedding as a last resort. The state of affairs continues to this day because neither there is a change in the attitude of glaciers nor a decrease in the use of air conditioning and fans.

During the period of Gen. Zia-ul-Haq in the office, through advertisement on the mainstream media, the government called for the mandatory helmet use by the riders of motorcycles and scooters; and vowed to impose a fine against those who did not comply. The government announced a deadline for riders to buy helmets before they would start penalizing the violators. The act triggered an overwhelming sale of helmets across the country; in the shops, by vendors, and even on stalls set up along the pavements. The period is remembered as the golden period for the traffic police department in the country who seemed to have struck it lucky. The police were spotted waiting for violators who would grease their palms and help them earn some pocket money. The process continued until stocks of helmets lasted in the market. It emerged later that one of Zia's close friends who had bought the stock from an international auction at a cheap price had asked the President for a favour in selling the helmets at a reasonable price. Zia-ul-Haq, a very caring friend indeed, came up with this legal and brilliant idea to help his friend earn some profit.

Pakistan is abundant with geniuses such as our rulers who are especially blessed to have fertile minds. They regularly invent novel schemes for benefiting themselves and their relatives. In 1992, such an idea occurred to the then-Prime Minister Nawaz Sharif who introduced a mind-blowing scheme called "Yellow Cab Scheme."[1] The project was aimed at providing the unemployed youth with jobs to help them make some decent income. But then, having no reputable automotive industry in the country, the government was left with no choice but to import thousands of cars from Korea to create job opportunities for the unemployed youth.

During the 90s, the government started promoting the use of CNG (Compressed Natural Gas) in vehicles. Through advertisements on the mainstream media, the government convinced the masses that petrol is imported from the international market, therefore it gobbles the country's foreign currency

[1] Farhan Bokhari, "Yellow Cab Scheme Hits Financial Hurdles", The Christian Science Monitor, September 01, 1993
Https://www.csmonitor.com/1993/0901/01092.html.

reserves. If the vehicles were fitted with CNG kits, not only would it help in cutting the cost but also improve the air quality and help the environment, which would ultimately have a positive impact on human lives. The scheme gained huge popularity and so did the factories that manufactured CNG kits mushroomed in the country. There was a time when about 80% of vehicles were converted to run on CNG and CNG refuelling stations proliferated throughout the country.[2] After around 2.5 million car owners converted their vehicles to run on CNG, then the government suddenly introduced strict rationing on the use of CNG. Explaining the reason, the government issued a statement that the country's natural gas reserves were on a decline, therefore, the motorists were directed to minimise the use of natural gas to ensure the unabated supply to the factories. Subsequently, the CNG refuelling stations remained closed for weeks. And when they reopened, long queues of motorists were formed waiting to refill their vehicles which forced the vehicle owners to switch back to petrol.

But the worst was yet to come. Despite a historic low in the global oil prices, the country has faced a grave shortage of petrol in the past few weeks.[3] In many cases, people were seen queuing outside petrol stations holding bottles to refill and men were spotted wearing *burkas* to get petrol. This reminded me of Zia-

[2] Aamir Shafaat Khan, "Duty, ST on CNG Kits to raise prices of cars", DAWN News, September 25, 2002,
https://www.dawn.com/news/58701/duty-st-on-cng-kits-to-raise-prices-of-cars.

[3] DAWN News, "Petrol crises: a very serious governance failure", DAWN News, January 27, 2015, Https://www.dawn.com/news/1159494.

ul-Haq whose golden policies still served as the beacons of light for the Pakistani rulers. Last year, the government introduced a similar scheme by the name of "Prime Minister Energy Saver Program" to address the country's energy crises.[*] To propagate the use of energy savers among the masses and help them benefit by the scheme, an extravagant amount of money was invested on advertisements. According to the government, the idea behind this program was to overcome the chronic electricity shortages. Therefore, around 30 million energy savers were distributed free to people throughout the country. It was intended to encourage people to use energy savers instead of regular bulbs. Suppose if one energy saver costs around hundred rupees, then it is easy to figure out that around three billion rupees worth of energy savers have been distributed. Despite all these efforts, the duration of load-shedding is on the rise. Now, only the government would be able to explain whom did they benefit by distributing free energy savers worth three billion rupees and by the extravagant advertisements?

These are just a few examples. A broader look on the events that occurred during the past few years clearly shows that from the "Sasti Roti Scheme" to the "Benazir Income Support Program," our politicians have left no stone unturned to help the poor masses. It is not hard to fathom that through these schemes, whether or not they have helped the poor masses, but

[*]Pakistan Live News, "Prime Minister Energy Saver Programme to overcome Electricity Load shedding", Pakistan Live News, December 17, 2013, https://news.paktron.net/2013/12/prime-minister-energy-saver-program-to.html.

they have certainly benefited their flesh and blood that are passionate about buying offshore properties at low prices. The poor, as yet, have got no access to the basic necessities such as food, clean water, electricity and gas. As far as the shortage of petrol is concerned, being a luxury item, it is hardly of any concern to the poor. Ironically, our rulers think that the poor masses only require the charity of one thousand rupees monthly from the "Benazir Income Support Program,"[5] to be able to benefit from Shehbaz Sharif's "Sasti Roti Scheme"[6] to keep body and soul together.

It is easy to conclude that while setting out the foundation of Pakistan, someone laid the first brick at a wrong angle that has resulted in permanent structural defects in the walls.

For such an occasion, Mevlana Jalal ad-Din Balkhi Rumi had said,

If you want to build your hose properly
Bewear to lay the foundations correctly,
Or else you'll get an unstable structure
That may fall to the ground eventuaaly.

The original article was published on DAWN Urdu website on February 05, 2015.

[5]Anwer Sumra, "Bitter truth about Sasti Roti", The Express TRIBUNE, November 28, 2010,
https://tribune.com.pk/story/82936/bitter-truth-about-sasti-roti.

[7]Hassan Riza Changezi, "ٹیڑھی اینٹ", DAWN Urdu, February 05, 2015,
https://www.dawnnews.tv/news/1016442/05feb2015-terhi-eent-hasan-raza-changezi-bm.

31

Hazara Genocide!
(Motives and Factors)

Much has been written about when and how the United States, with the help of Saudi Arabia and Pakistan's Inter-Services Intelligence (ISI), initiated a war against the Soviet Union in Afghanistan. I, for one, believe that Zia-ul-Haq's military coup, Zulfikar Ali Bhutto's dismissal, and the latter's subsequent execution was not an internal job, but part of a more complex international conspiracy aimed at preventing the spread of socialism and the Soviet influence in the region. In fact, the narrative of Islamic Jihad was used as a motive to achieve the very same goal. The prime objective was to assemble all the mercenaries from around the world and get them to fight the Soviet Union. Without being tagged as the army of a specific country, those private contractors would serve to achieve the goals set by the US.

Obviously, the American, Pakistani and Saudi Arabian rulers and their agencies were well cognizant of the fact that the road to paradise did not pass-through Afghanistan. Yet, they did know that motives of defending the religion, the war against the infidels and atheists, the greed for reward and the longing for paradise, and the company of 72 virgins in the hereafter, were tempting enough to persuade ordinary Muslims to participate in jihad. Therefore, the US dollars and Saudi riyals funnelled to Pakistan to help ease its borders allowing the influx of *mujahedeen*[1] from across the world and a holy war was declared against the infidel Soviet Union. Although, the first and foremost aim of this jihad was to contain the influence of socialism and the Soviet Union that posed a big threat to the American capitalism and its superiority in the region, Pakistan, Saudi Arabia and Iran as the benefactors of the war, were equally busy picking up the fruits of the American version of the holy war. In the past, Pakistani officials had always accused the Afghan leaders for not only supporting but also funding the separatist movements in Pakistan. Therefore, if a Pakistan friendly government was established in Afghanistan in the wake of this jihad, it would significantly help Pakistan to overcome one of its greatest problems. On the other hand, Iran and Saudi Arabia, the self-proclaimed torchbearers of two different but opposing denominations of Islam, had always been engaged in undermining one another and establishing their hegemony in the region along with the aim of accomplishing the American dream. Unfortunately, their struggle for gaining dominance did not remain restricted to Afghanistan and it was just

[1]The plural form of *mujahid*, the Arabic term for one engaged in jihad

a matter of time before it engulfed other countries in the region and beyond. With the support from General Zia-ul-Haq, politically as well as ideologically closer to Saudi Arabia, it became possible for Saudi regime to easily influence the Sunni militant groups in Afghanistan. Likewise, Iran kept showing its extended support for the Shia militant groups. This tug of war between the two rival forces resulted in the rise of sectarian violence in Afghanistan and Pakistan. In the years that followed, Pakistani society witnessed a surge in the formation of sectarian based religious organizations. This sectarian climate triggered the formation of Tehrek-e-Nifaz-e-Fiqh-Jafaria (TNJP) (Movement for Promulgation of Shiite Jurisprudence) which demanded the government to impose *Jafari Fiqh* (Shiite Jurisprudence) on national level.[2] During the period of 1985, the demonstrations held by TNJP against the government to fulfil their demands, played a pivotal role in intensifying the sectarian violence in the country. Following on their footsteps, various sectarian groups originated to claim their communal rights from the government.

Allama Ehsan Elahi Zaheer became the first target of the sectarian conflict in Pakistan.[3] Adherent of the Al-Hadith sect of Islam, he was known for his stance against the Barelvis and Shiite denominations of Islam and was very critical of the Jamaat-e-Islami. He even opposed the Sharia Bill of Zia-Ul-Haq and was strongly

---

[2] GlobalSecurity.org, Tehrik-Nifaz-e-Fiqh-e-Jafaria (TNFJ), July 09, 2018, https://www.globalsecurity.org/military/world/para/tjp.htm.

[3] Ayesha Umar, "Kill, in the name of religion", The Express TRIBUNE, June 15, 2011,
https://tribune.com.pk/article/6439/kill-in-the-name-of-religion.

disliked by him. He was targeted on March 30, 1987 in a bomb blast while addressing a rally. Reportedly the bomb was planted in a flowerpot placed on the stage. Fourteen people who were believed to be the followers of Al-Hadith and Salafi sects were killed in the incident. Ehsan Elahi Zaheer got injured in the incident and was taken to Riyadh, Saudi Arabia, for treatment where he died in a hospital.[4] His followers directly blamed Iran for his death and in vengeance they bombed a car in Punjab which was reportedly carrying the Iranian engineers.

Although the sectarian terrorism in Pakistan took roots during the period of General Zia-ul-Haq, the self-proclaimed commander of the faithful, but significantly flourished during the first term of Nawaz Sharif as the prime minister. In a bid to end the sectarian war, Nawaz Sharif tried to unite Shia and Sunni scholars. He urged them to work together for bringing sectarian harmony by adhering to the policy of peaceful co-existence and refrain from humiliating and blasphemous remarks about other sects. He was more or less successful in achieving this goal and around thirty scholars and religious figures signed the agreement under the title of Ittehad-e-Bain-ul-Muslimeen Committee (Committee for Unity Among the Muslims). In 1992, after the agreement was signed, the graph of sectarian violence in Punjab clearly showed a rapid decline. However, by that time, the conflict had already spilled to the other provinces of Pakistan.

---

[4]Sabir Shah, "Notables killed in Lahore in six decades", The News, February 14, 2017, https://www.thenews.com.pk/print/186187-Notables-killed-in-Lahore-in-six-decades.

In 1997, when Nawaz Sharif was elected as the prime minister for a second time by winning a two third majority, once again Punjab was facing the threats of sectarian war. His brother Shehbaz Sharif was elected as the chief minister of Punjab. On his special instructions, many criminals involved in sectarian killings were arrested and a large number was killed in police encounters. It was clearly done to avoid the lengthy and weak court trials for bringing the criminals to justice. However, the process came to an end when in 1999 Nawaz Sharif nearly escaped a car bomb explosion near Raiwind.[5] Lashkar-e-Jhangvi accepted the responsibility for the attack. After the incident the Sharif Brothers were left with no option but to sign an agreement with the terrorist supporters to release the criminals who were imprisoned. As a result, the terrorists exited Punjab and established their strongholds in other parts of the country particularly in Quetta and Karachi. In those days, news was circulating that some active members of Lashkar-e-Jhangvi in Punjab had sent bangles to their fellow mujahideen in Quetta as a symbol of cowardice to shame them. This was clearly an attempt to incite them to kill the apostates and resume their activities. In the following year, people in Quetta witnessed the first incident of sectarian violence when Sardar Nisar Ali, a Hazara leader, was targeted in a deadly attack.[6] He was badly injured while his driver and guard both lost their

[5]Suzanne Goldenberg, "Pakistani PM escapes bomb blast", The Guardian, January 04, 1999,
https://www.theguardian.com/world/1999/jan/04/suzannegoldenberg.

[6]Akhlaq Ullah Tarar, "Targeted killing of Hazaras", DAWN News, November 12, 2018, https://www.dawn.com/news/1445093.

lives in the attack. It must be remembered that the terrorist behind the attack belonged to Punjab who was sent on a special mission to Quetta to carry out the attack. In fact, this incident was an attempt to expel sectarianism from Punjab to Balochistan and Sindh. It was believed to be part of the agreement between the Sharif brothers and the Lashkar-e-Jhangvi.

According to the statistics of Hazara Organisation for Peace and Equality (HOPE), from October 1999 to date, around 158 terrorist attacks have been carried out on the Hazara community in Quetta which has claimed the lives of 1400 people which include men, women and children.[7] Meanwhile, the number of wounded, many with permanent disabilities, is around 3500. What are the factors behind these attacks that have spanned over the last one and a half decade? Are they a part of a complex international plan? Are these massacres sectarian in nature? Is it actually part of the plan to rid the region of Shias? Or is the sectarianism used as a cover to secure actual targets? In other words, is the conflict a consequence of Iranian and Saudi proxy war for establishing their hegemony in the region? Or is this an attempt by the government to divert the attention of the world away from the Baloch separatist movement by using Hazaras as scapegoats? Has the government actually failed to stop these terrorists or is the government secretly backing them? Is the law-and-order situation really improving or is it going to deteriorate rapidly all over the country including Quetta? In such circumstances what should we do?

Hazara.net, Hazara Organisation for Peace and Equality, 2013,

http://www.hazara.net/hope/.

These are the questions which require a detailed discussion.

For a long time, I had been thinking about writing on this subject but due to a number of reasons, I had not been able to. The significance and vastness of the subject demand a detailed discussion. As a preface, I have expressed my take on the subject. I would try to share my thoughts on the subject with my readers step by step.

International Conspiracy

After the completion of Soviet withdrawal from Afghanistan on 15 February 1989 and the subsequent victory of Afghan mujahideen, the US had apparently achieved success in the first step of this plan. At that time, a largely discussed conspiracy theory under the title of the new world order was very popular. The theory was based on the idea of making collective efforts in the future to counter the expansionism of a powerful country such as the Soviet Union which could pose a threat to the US. Therefore, it became mandatory to develop new policies and strategies to weaken those countries that were capable of building nuclear weapons and were militarily and economically stable by dismembering them into pieces, so that in future they would not remain a threat to the US interests.

In December 1991, with the disintegration of the Soviet Union and the dissolution of the former superpower into fifteen independent states, the decades-long cold war came to an end. Subsequently, the US and its allies began to modify their policies and strategies to cope with the new world map. A statement by the NATO commander stirred up a lot of controversy stating Islam and Islamic extremism a threat for the existing world peace and called for strategies to curb them. Now, if we believe in this conspiracy theory and regard the NATO commander's statement as a policy of the west, then we must analyse the events that occurred over the past decades from that perspective.

On September 11, 2001, after the terrorist attacks on the twin towers in New York, the US immediately put the blame on the Islamic extremists fighting the holy war in Afghanistan during the past few years. In response to the attacks, the US with the help of the UK invaded Afghanistan using advanced weaponry to bring the criminals and their supporters to justice. Shortly afterwards, the US with the help of anti-Taliban groups deposed the Taliban and its allies from Afghanistan. In the process, thousands of the Taliban fighters were killed, and a large number was arrested. Those who fled took refuge in Pakistan and the tribal areas of Pakistan became a safe haven for them. As a result, the well-trained Taliban warriors who included a large number of sectarian terrorists initiated a never-ending chain of target killings and suicide bombings under the cover of sectarian hatred and religious extremism. During this period, not only top military institutions were targeted, and law enforcers were killed, but also, mosques, madrassas, religious centres, shrines, mausoleums and public places were bombed. These terror incidents are estimated to have taken the lives of more than fifty thousand innocent citizens.

In 2009, the then-governor of Khyber Pakhtunkhwa (KP), Owais Ahmed Ghani revealed in his interview that the monthly expenditures of the extremist groups active in tribal areas of Pakistan is around 2 billion rupees which included their wages, housing, food, transport, ammunition, and expenses of the families of the martyrs. Replying to a question about the source of income supporting the terrorist groups, he stated, "The income is generated by the trade of opium which is cultivated in Afghanistan." The question arises here is whether the Taliban have the possession of such lands to cultivate opium? Aren't they engaged in a guerrilla war? In the presence of NATO forces in Afghanistan, if opium is cultivated on a large scale generating a sizable income financing the militants in Pakistan, then isn't it a matter of concern for Pakistan?

After travelling thousands of miles and crossing many borders, thousands of fighters from Yemen, Sudan, Egypt, Algeria, Iraq, Libya, Jordan, Tunis, Saudi Arabia, Syria and other gulf countries entered Pakistan during the past decade to start a crusade. Instead of choosing to build good relations with the neighbouring countries of Palestine and Lebanon and assist them in waging a war against Israel to free *Bait-ul-Muqaddas* (Jerusalem),[8] why did they prefer to come to Pakistan and Afghanistan and kill innocent citizens? What could be the reasons behind the permanent stay of the Chechen fighters in the tribal areas who, instead of fighting Russia to free their country, chose to stay in Pakistan? Likewise, instead of fighting their

---

[8]Al-Aqsa Mosque in the old city of Jerusalem

government, why the Uzbek fighters chose to build ties with the international networks and are fighting against Pakistani citizens and institutions? The Chinese mujahideen who receive training in our tribal areas to run separatist movements in various provinces of China and who are believed to be involved in various terrorist incidents, whose agenda are they following? Carrying out suicide attacks, bombing religious places of different sects, the targeted killings of religious and political leaders, bombings in crowded public places, targeted attacks on law enforcement forces, inciting religious hatred and vicious killings of innocent citizens in Pakistan, one is forced to think as to how are they retaliating the American army and its allies? On the contrary, people who want to put Pakistan on the brink of disintegration, instability, and civil war, are actually the ones who are working to put this well-known conspiracy theory into practice.

The political landscape in Iraq offers almost the same view. In response to the 9/11 attacks, when the American tanks rolled into Iraq in early 2003, the US and its allies gave three reasons for invading the country. To overthrow Saddam's regime which was accused of supporting international terrorism, destruction of WMD (weapons of mass destruction) and the liberation of Iraqis. After executing President Saddam Hussein and establishing a government of their choice, the Bush administration confessed that they had failed to locate any WMD. In the aftermath of this war, numerous militant groups mushroomed in the Iraqi society causing hundreds of thousands Iraqi lives in the violence, bombings, suicide bombings, rocket attacks and mass killings.

According to the statistics, since the start of the war in Iraq, as many as 1.3 million Iraqis were estimated to have been killed in the period between June 2003 and 2009, whereas the number of allied forces, who were killed in the war, was around four thousand roughly.[9] Some sources claim the number of civilian fatalities to be around 2.5 million. In fact, a large number of deaths were not caused directly by the coalition forces but by the sectarian and religious extremists. By igniting a civil war and inciting Iraqis to fight each other, these sectarian groups provided the external forces with the opportunity to rule on them and loot their wealth. By diverting people's attention from Palestine and Israel, they forced them in a never-ending cycle of sectarian war.

It is to be noted that in 2009, the new government formed under the leadership of President Obama announced a complete withdrawal of the US troops from Iraq by 2011 and pledged to form a government according to the will of Iraqis.[10] Meanwhile, he approved an increase in the number of armed forces deployed in Afghanistan. Following the change of strategy by the US, Al-Qaeda leaders in Iraq directed

---

[9] Philip Bump, "15 years after Iraq War began, the death toll is still murky", The Washington Post, March 20, 2018,

https://www.washingtonpost.com/news/politics/wp/2018/03/20/15-years-after-it-began-the-death-toll-from-the-iraq-war-is-still-murky/.

[10] BBC News, "All US troops to leave Iraq in 2011", BBC News, October 21, 2011,

https://www.bbc.co.uk/news/world-us-canada-15410154.

their fighters to leave Iraq and take refuge in Afghanistan and tribal areas of Pakistan. In the following days, the western media repeatedly broadcast such news and analysis describing Pakistan to be more dangerous than Iraq and Afghanistan and urged the US administration to draw their attention from Iraq and Afghanistan and focus on the nuclear power Pakistan that is posing a greater threat to world peace. The statements issued by US officials showing their concerns on the upsurge of terrorist activities in Pakistan and the risk of Pakistan's nuclear weapons falling into the wrong hands, are on the record.[11] If we believe in conspiracy theory regarding the new world order, then the ongoing violence in Tunis, Libya, Egypt, Syria, Pakistan and Afghanistan must also be seen in the same perspective. Particularly in a situation when the news of the US supporting the opposition forces in Tunis, Libya, Egypt and Syria is spreading like wildfire. Likewise, if we believe in the accusations that the world powers are conspiring against the sole Islamic nuclear power and have plans to disintegrate it, then we must consider the incidents happening in Waziristan to Karachi and the separatist movement in Balochistan as part and parcel of the international conspiracy theory. To accomplish this goal, the Hazaras like every other ethnic minority group are burned as fuel to help this fire grow. But would it be perfectly fine to think along these lines?

BBC News, "Clinton warns on Pakistan threat", BBC News, October 11, 2009, http://news.bbc.co.uk/1/hi/world/europe/8301249.stm.

Interference by India

It is a recognised fact that prosperity and development of a country largely depend on the law-and-order situation. It would not be wrong to say that due to the decades-long violence and ever-growing lawlessness in the country, the state has failed to maintain its writ on various internal affairs causing people to lose faith in the state. The prevailing anarchy in the country has resulted in the foreign investment to come to a standstill as well as to the exodus of local investors. Institutions are on the verge of collapse and the country is going through the economic crisis that is not hidden from anyone. Pakistan's old rival India is taking full advantage of this crisis. Not only is India gaining economic stability by leaps and bounds but also working hard to establish its hegemony in the region. Both countries have a history of mutual distrust accusing each other of interfering in each other's internal affairs. India has frequently accused Pakistan of masterminding the December 2001 attack on the Indian parliament[12] and the 2008 Mumbai attacks[13] while Pakistan has openly blamed India for creating anarchy and violence on its soil.[14] Pakistani circles

---

[12]Abhinav Bhatt, "India slams Pakistan as Parliament attack mastermind resurfaces, calls for 'jihad'", NDTV, February 22, 2014, https://www.ndtv.com/india-news/india-slams-pakistan-as-parliament-attack-mastermind-resurfaces-calls-for-jihad-551532.

[13]BBC News, "Mumbai attack gunman Ajmal qasab executed", BBC News, November 21, 2012, https://www.bbc.co.uk/news/world-asia-india-20422265.

[14]M Ilyas Khan, "What lies behind Pakistani charges of Indian 'terrorism'", BBC News, May 06, 2015, https://www.bbc.co.uk/news/world-asia-32604137

strongly believe that India is funding the separatist movement in Balochistan and even accuse the Indian representations in Afghanistan for creating a state of lawlessness and anarchy in Pakistan.

There is no denying the fact that Pakistan has always considered its eastern neighbour, India its biggest enemy. Iran is situated on the western border and China, on the northeast. Pakistan has always maintained friendly relations with both these countries. Pakistan's relationship with Afghanistan, on the other hand, has experienced fluctuations at different times. Pakistan struggled hard to obtain nuclear capability, primarily in response to the development of nuclear weapons by its old rival, India. In May 1998, when Pakistan carried out its first atomic test in Chaghai, it was in response to the nuclear test conducted by India, a week earlier, in Pokhran.

The purpose of recalling these incidents is that many analysts blame Pakistan's cordial relations with China and its hostile relations with India as the reasons for the state of lawlessness and the Hazara genocide in Balochistan. They hold the arguement that the geographic importance of the Gwadar port and its lease to China are matters of concern to both India and America. Some factions even blame this tug of war between the two neighbouring countries for inflaming the Baloch separatist movement. In my opinion the rising interest and influence of China in Balochistan is not directly linked to Hazara killings but it might have affected our lives indirectly. I will try to discuss this point in the later sections of the essay.

Iran-Saudi proxy war

Iran-Saudi struggle for regional influence is a common factor for the Hazara genocide or more suitably this proxy war is regarded as one of the major contributing factors behind the ongoing Hazara genocide. Some try to summarise the debate by accusing these countries' long sectarian wars for the Hazara genocide. As I mentioned earlier that this sectarian war is tactfully used in contemporary times to cover for the economic and political gains which are the actual objectives of this proxy war. Therefore, in my opinion the objective of the Arab-Iran proxy war is the same. To fully comprehend the nature of this indirect conflict happening over the past four decades, we need to have a close look on the successive events that occurred in the past.

The Iranian revolution took place at a time when the Pakistani society was under the strong grip of Zia's dictatorship. The holy war was in the offing against the communist regime in Afghanistan. After the victory of Islamic revolution in Iran, many slogans became popular including "Islam has no boundaries." Actually, it was not just a slogan but a reflection of the aspirations of Iranian mullahs to export Iranian revolution to other parts of the world. If their wish remained restricted to just a slogan, it would not have caused much concern to Iranian rivals. However, it was soon transformed into an ideology and the Iranian leaders sought to extend their sphere of influence to countries outside Iran particularly Pakistan which led their Arab rivals to announce their participation in this war. It was not a mere coincidence that just months after the Iranian revolution, Tehrek-e-Nifaz-e-fiqh-e-Jafaria, a Shia organisation was formed in Pakistan that demanded the government to impose Jafari Fiqh in the country and also raised the slogans for initiating a similar version of Iranian revolution in Pakistan. Back then, the Arab Jihadists were arriving in both Pakistan and Afghanistan supposedly to participate in the war against the Soviet Union. Simultaneously, with the support of Middle Eastern countries, training camps under the guise of religious seminaries began to appear throughout Pakistan, to train the jihadists. The process of funding various sectarian forces also commenced. The Arab fighters who came to stay in Pakistan for longer periods brought their whole families along with them. In order to mingle with the local population and win their trust, they would marry their daughters to the locals and support them financially. Apparently, this was the formal start of the proxy war between Saudi and Iran on Pakistani soil.

The period of 1985 is an important chapter in Pakistan's sectarian history. Tehrek-e-Nifaz-e-Fiqh-e-Jafaria began holding demonstrations throughout the country demanding the establishment of Jafari Fiqha in Pakistan. Then Allama Arif Hussain Hussaini was the president of the organisation. He was a close friend of the Iranian Supreme Leader Ayatollah Khomeini. During a similar protest in Quetta, some local mullahs threatened the government that if their demands were not fulfilled, they would not hesitate to turn Quetta into another Lebanon. Lebanon was, then, going through an intense civil war between numerous militant groups. The threats made by Iran-returned mullahs really meant they were ready to push Quetta into a civil war. As a result of the hate speeches by mullahs, violence broke out during the rally turning it into a bloody protest which claimed the lives of innocent citizens including some police cadets.[15] Some people termed it Shia-Sunni clashes, while Zia's-controlled media also played a crucial role in fanning the flames which resulted in increased gaps between various sects and communities. This incident provided an excuse to Saudi Arabia and the Middle Eastern countries to strengthen their favourite groups.

On 6 September 1985, two months after July 6, Anjuman-e-Sipah-e-Sahaba (ASS) was founded in the Punjab town of Jhang, in Pakistan.[16] The prime objective of this organisation was to counter the growing influence of Iranian revolution and Shiism in Pakistan. I mentioned earlier in the essay that Allama Ehsan Elahi Zaheer was the first victim of sectarian conflict whose death was directly blamed on Iran.[17] A few weeks after his death, a bus carrying the Iranian engineers was hit by an explosion. The incident was

[15] Malik Siraj Akbar, "Hazara tribesmen under attack", Hazara International, February 06, 2009,
https://www.hazarapeople.com/2009/02/06/hazara-tribesmen-under-attack-in-quetta/.

[16] Mapping Militant Organizations, Sipah-e-Sahaba Pakistan, February 15, 2012,
https://web.stanford.edu/group/mappingmilitants/cgi-bin/groups/view/147#attacks.

[17] Sabir Shah, "Notables killed in Lahore in six decades", The News, February 14, 2017,
https://www.thenews.com.pk/print/186187-Notables-killed-in-Lahore-in-six-decades.

reported to be an act of retaliation for Alama Zaheer's murder. Consequently, Pakistan entered a cycle of sectarian violence. On 5 August 1988, Allama Arif Hussain Hussaini was killed.[18] In February 1990, Haq Nawaz Jhangvi, the founder of Anjuman-e-Sipah-e-Sahaba which was later renamed as Sipah-e-Sahaba Pakistan (SSP), was gunned down.[19] As a reaction in December 1990, Sadeq Ganji, the Director of Iran-Pakistan Cultural Center was killed in a targeted attack in Lahore.[20] The unabated killings continued for more than a decade in Punjab. During this time Sipah-e-Sahaba gave rise to its offshoots Lashkar-e-Jhangvi while Sipah-e-Mohammad emerged as an offshoot of Tehrek-e-Nifaz-e-Fiqh-e-Jafaria. Together the duo initiated a chain of unprecedented sectarian killings in Punjab which claimed the lives of many engineers, doctors, businessmen, teachers and ordinary citizens, majority of whom were the adherents of the Shia sect of Islam. During this time, a large number of educated and professional factions of society along with the businessmen were forced to leave Pakistan and migrate to other countries resulting in the outflow of capital from Punjab to other provinces as well as other countries. Finally, the Sharif brothers decided to enter negotiations with Lashkar-e-Jhangvi and sign an

[18]Ayesha Umar, "Kill, in the name of religion", The Express TRIBUNE, June 15, 2011,
https://tribune.com.pk/article/6439/kill-in-the-name-of-religion.

[19]IBID

[20]Sabir Shah, "Notables killed in Lahore in six decades", The News, February 14, 2017,
https://www.thenews.com.pk/print/186187-Notables-killed-in-Lahore-in-six-decades.

agreement. As a result, all the terrorist groups including Lashkar-e-Jhangvi stood banned in Punjab and were redirected to regions in Balochistan and Karachi. Lashkar-e-Jhangvi, initially, chose the Baloch areas located near the Regional Cooperation for Development (RCD) Highway, a famous international route connecting Pakistan to Iran. This region has always been a focal point of interest to Iran. To enhance its influence in the region, Iran has always paid special attention to the tribes living there. As a result, in 1990, there was a clear rise in the number of people converting to Shia Islam. It was rumoured that a few prominent Baloch figures living in Mastung, and neighbouring areas were likely to convert to Shia sect of Islam. Some families even did so. When the terrorist groups involved in sectarian violence moved there, they chose Mastung as their primary target. After making a strong foothold there, they started killing those families who had converted to the Shia sect. They killed those families brutally and mercilessly and prohibited the inhabitants of the area to hold funerals and offer their final rituals. It was a grim reminder to those who were involved in facilitating the Shia uprising and subsequent Iranian influence in the region.

To fully understand the Saudi-Iran proxy war in Pakistan, which is carried out under the cover of sectarianism, it is essential to have a look at the relations and policies of these three countries. Syed Ahmed Irshad Tirmizi, a former director of ISI, in his book, "The Sensitive Institutions" (Profiles of

Intelligence), page 268, has shed some light on Saudi Arabia's policies regarding Pakistan and Shias in these words, "The relation between Saudi and Shias regarding their faith and sect has always been cold. As a result, every government in Pakistan has accepted it as unwritten law and a vital part of their foreign policy. Where possible, they do not appoint any Shia diplomat in the Pakistani Embassy in Saudi Arabia. Nor do they deploy any Shia military personnel to Saudi Arabia for training purposes or any other military exercises.

To keep their hold on the country, Saudi rulers often grant Pakistan extensive financial aid in the form of oil worth billions of rupees.[21] Iran too adopted a similar policy. In 1998, when the Nawaz government conducted the nuclear tests, economic sanctions were imposed on Pakistan, and then Iran was the only country that stepped in to offer relief in repayment of loans and assured financial aid. It was believed to be part of a deal between Pakistan and Iran. According to the deal, Pakistan was bound to aid Iran with her atomic nuclear program[22] while Iran, in return, promised to assist Pakistan in gaining control over the central and northern areas of Afghanistan. It is to be noted that Pakistan performed its nuclear tests in May 1998. Roughly after three months, in August 1998, Taliban successfully gained control over Mazar-e-

---

[21]Khaleeq Kiani, "$15 billion Saudi bailout likely", DAWN News, May 23, 2013, https://www.dawn.com/news/1013070/15-billion-saudi-bailout-likely.

[22]Dean Nelson, "A.Q.Khan boasts of helping Iran's nuclear programme", The Telegraph, September 10, 2009,
https://www.telegraph.co.uk/news/worldnews/asia/pakistan/6170145/A.Q.-Khan-boasts-of-helping-Irans-nuclear-programme.html

Sharif. The attack, which lasted no longer than two days, led to the deaths of around eight thousand Hazara men, women, and children.[23] On August 08, when the Taliban advanced to Mazar-e-Sharif and captured the Iranian consulate, they killed nine Iranian Diplomats[24] and a journalist of Islamic Republic News Agency (IRNA). Responding to the incident, the Iranian President Akbar Hashemi Rafsanjani, in his statement, complained to Pakistan that this was not part of the deal. Accusing Pakistan of the incident, Iran demanded an inquiry whereas, Pakistan denied the allegations and blamed a Taliban affiliated group that was believed to be against the cordial relations between Pakistan and Iran. It was later revealed that Lashkar-e-Jhangvi was involved in the incident which is known to be against a friendly relation between Pakistan and Iran.

According to various investigative reports frequently published in Pakistani and international media, both Saudi Arabia and Iran are involved in funding and supporting their favourite militant groups in Pakistan. According to WikiLeaks, Saudi Arabia and other Gulf countries are involved in funding the madrassas in southern Punjab with million dollars in aid[25] while Iran is responsible for funding the Shia

[23]Dexter Filkins, "Afghan reports ethnic massacre by Taliban", Los Angeles Times, September 18, 1998, https://www.latimes.com/archives/la-xpm-1998-sep-18-mn-24021-story.html.

[24]Douglas Jehl, "Iran Holds Taliban Responsible for 9 Diplomats' Death", The New York Times, September 11, 1998,

https://www.nytimes.com/1998/09/11/world/iran-holds-taliban-responsible-for-9-diplomats-deaths.html.

militant groups. Both countries see themselves as the leaders of Shia and Sunni sects of Islam and are rich in oil and gas reserves. The revenues generated by the Hajj and other pilgrimages are in addition for which we have no data available. It is speculated that American economy is supported by billions of dollars of Saudi rulers. There are widespread stories of the Arab princes, allegedly spending millions of dollars on their lavish lifestyle in just a matter of hours.[26] One Saudi prince, for instance, even bought a property in Switzerland worth sixty million dollars. To get unique mobile phone numbers and car number plates, Arab princes would spend billions in auctions. On the other hand, according to international media, Iranian Supreme Leader Ayatollah Ali Khamenei owns a business empire worth millions of dollars.[27] In order to secure their economic and political interests and to perpetuate their influence in the region, if they spend a few billion dollars and kill a few thousand innocent citizens, then it is not a big deal for them.

It is worth mentioning that there are two types of

[25]Michael Busch, "WikiLeaks: Saudi-financed Madrassas More Widespread in Pakistan Than Thought", Foreign Policy in Focus, Focal Points, May 26, 2011,

https://fpif.org/wikileaks_saudi-financed_madrassas_more_widespread_in_pakistan_than_thought/.

[26]Jayne Clark, "Saudi Prince drops $20 million in Disney spending spree", USA Today, June 07, 2013,

https://eu.usatoday.com/story/dispatches/2013/06/07/disney-paris-saudi-prince/2402217/.

[27]Steve Stecklow, Debak Dehghanpisheh and Yeganeh Torbati, "Khamenei controls massive financial empire built on property seizures", Reuters Investigates, November 11, 2013,

https://www.reuters.com/investigates/iran/#article/part1.

Shia followers in Pakistan. The first type comprises the scholars who follow the Iraqi *Mujtahids*[28] (the highest religious scholar) and the second type are those who follow the Iranian *Mujtahids*. The former, generally spend their time studying and researching and refrain from participating in politics while the latter by contrast, takes great interest in politics. I personally know a few Hazara mullahs who had studied in Iraq. However, after the Iranian revolution, when the leaders sought to export their revolution and as a result achieved great financial gains, the Hazara mullahs changed their direction and started taking an active role in politics. By carrying the placards displaying the photos of Khomeini, they embarked on a similar journey. While on the other hand, many contemporary Hazara mullahs who had studied in Najaf were always engaged in studying and teaching and never took an active role in politics. Nor did they try to use Khomeini's photos as a cover to gain financial benefits. By contrast, Iran-returned mullahs always carried placards displaying the photos of Khomeini, Khamenei, and Rafsanjani. Moreover, they have the honour of introducing the Lebanese Shia leader Hassan Nasrullah to the Hazara Community in Quetta who is believed to be an Iranian proxy in Lebanon. Apparently, if it was the matter of faith, these Shia scholars would give the same level of respect to the Iraqi scholars. But it is clearly

---

[28] (Singular is Mujtahid) an individual who is qualified to exercise ijtihad in the evaluation of Islamic law

[29] CNN, "Death toll from Pakistan suicide bombing rises to 73", CNN, September 04, 2010,
https://edition.cnn.com/2010/WORLD/asiapcf/09/03/pakistan.violence/index.html.

obvious from their processions, congregations, characters and statements that they are using religion to cover their activities in accomplishing the Iranian agenda. Take the example of Quds Day (Jerusalem Day) which is solely an Iranian agenda. But the mullahs, who work for promoting the Iranian interests, celebrate this day with great enthusiasm every year. In 2010, at Mizan Choke in Quetta, a suicide bomber exploded himself during Quds Day procession claiming the lives of more than 100 innocent citizens.[29]

Groups like Lashkar-i-Jhanghvi, Jaysh al-Islam and the organisation that serves as their mouthpiece in the media, the Ahle Sunnat Wal Jamaat, have repeatedly denied holding any resentment towards the Hazara Community, however, they have openly expressed hostility against those who have been trained by Iran or those involved in the printing of blasphemous literature. But they have constantly failed to provide single evidence that proves the involvement of any Hazara in any terrorist activity. Nor could they present a blasphemous literature printed or written by any Hazara. It is crystal clear that all the sectarian content against any sect is usually printed and published in other provinces particularly in Punjab. The merciless killings of Hazaras prove one point that both groups involved in the proxy war are actually following the agendas of their supporters by killing Hazaras and using religion as a cover for their actions.

---

[29]CNN, "Death toll from Pakistan suicide bombing rises to 73", CNN, September 04, 2010,

https://edition.cnn.com/2010/WORLD/asiapcf/09/03/pakistan.violence/index.html.

During the previous government, the former interior minister Rehman Malik, in his briefing to the cabinet, mentioned the possible involvement of two Islamic brotherly countries for the ongoing violence in Pakistan, in general and Quetta, in particular. Responding to a question regarding this topic, the former foreign minister, Hina Rabbani Khar, said that the foreign protocol did not allow them to name the two countries. It is to be noted that in 2001-2002, during Pervez Musharraf's reign, the sectarian groups that were banned in Pakistan were not dealt with the iron hands due to the fears of a possible outrage by the two brother Islamic countries, some media sources claim.

According to an estimate, Hazaras make up around 0.2% of the total 180million population[30] in Pakistan. Meanwhile, the Shias constitute between 20-25% of the country's total population. The largest number of Shias reside in Punjab which, in turn, is the most populated province of Pakistan. During the last one and a half decades, more than fourteen hundred Hazaras have fallen victim to terrorism, a relatively large number with regard to their small population. If we have a look at the statistics of the last fifteen years, it is easy to perceive that during the last decade, the maximum number of terrorist incidents happened in Balochistan which is the least populated province having the least Shia inhabitants. More than 90% of the victims of these incidents are the Hazaras which include a large number of women and children.

---

[30]Hazara.net, Hazara Organisation for Peace and Equality, 2013, http://www.hazara.net/hope/.

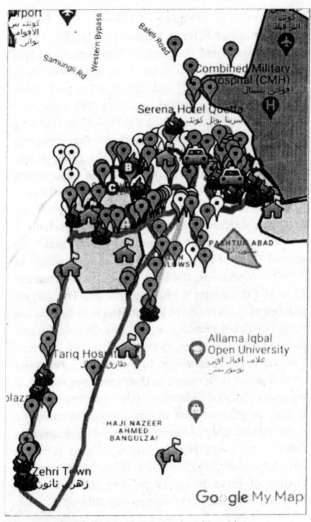

The map pinpoints the attacked locations on the Hazaras in and around Quetta, Pakistan.
Source: Hazara Organization for Peace and Equality (HOPE)
Twitter: http://www.twitter.com/HOPEHazara

Book Review

Unfinished Stories- The Tales of Unfinished Lives

Unfinished Stories is an English translation of Hassan Raza Changezi's book, Qisahai Na Thamam, which narrates the tales of unfinished lives, victimized by religious terrorism in Pakistan; particularly, of the Hazara community members, living in Quetta, the capital of Balochistan province. The stories and essays in the book relate to all the persecuted members of the community. They tell the tales of the children whose bodies were torn apart before they could grow to fulfill their dreams or those of their parents; they talk of the youngsters who were massacred before they could get any chance to pursue the careers of their choice or to start families with the life partners they had dreamt of; they recount the stories of the parents whose lives were cut short before they could gather enough money to put their children in the universities of their choice or to see them prosper in their professions; and they are also the tragedies of those who suffer from trauma and depression after they have lost their beloved family members or friends. They truly are the unfinished stories, the stories of the lives that could not be lived and the dreams that could not be realized.

Hassan Raza Changezi does not only narrate these stories (written between 2013 to 2017), but also draws a sketch of the overall socio-political context, wherein these stories originate, evolve, and thrive. He, analytically and satirically, links this context with the deeds of the authoritative junta in Pakistan, the military-civil and religious leaders who have turned the country into a 'lab', by performing 'failed experiments' since its independence. Unfortunately, the repercussions of these experiments, Changezi believes, are borne by the common people, especially the minority communities; therefore, they are the ones who face discrimination, negligence, and above all misery. Notably, he unmasks the true face of the ruling junta with laudable courage and determination though the space for freedom of speech in Pakistan has always remained cramped, and the audible voices have always faced severe consequences.

Changezi, in no way, evades any criticism of people's docility towards their leaders either that paves the way for such experiments to be performed unperturbed. He also censures duplicity among the people and their indifferent behavior that ignores the social evils, or in certain cases, even invigorates them. Extending his criticism, he approaches the media in Pakistan, condemning it for having no appreciable role to project the audible voices mentioned above, but creating a noise that has outvoiced the echoes of truth, the whining of social evils, and the cries of the needy. In his essay the 'Opportunistic Flip-floppers in Pakistani Media' he unleashes his criticism on the journalists and media houses who have prioritized material gains over the dissemination of facts and truth. In another essay, he denounces the social media users for turning the platform into a 'public toilet'.

In the context mentioned above, Changezi opines, the rights of the underprivileged sections of the society remain discriminated, and their voices remain muffled. He, appropriately, presents the case of Balochistan in this regard. The province as a whole has remained neglected by the central government, while the politicians at the provincial level are hand-picked by the ruling junta to keep even the rightful public demands overlooked. Such a suffocating environment has led to an unrest and militancy, which is getting out of proportions, and the authorities, having no solution to offer, have decided to cover it by giving a free rein to Takfiri terrorism, and targeted killings of Hazaras in the province. While the countries like Iran and Saudi Arabia, finding an open ground for a proxy war, take advantage of the situation. Obviously, the severest of the outcomes have befallen on the Hazara community as they have faced all sorts of terrorism from individual targeted attacks to mass-killings, which include two major incidents on Alamdar Road and Hazara Town in early 2013, each killing around 100 people and injuring as many.

Much to the chagrin of the community, some of the relevant authorities and fellow citizens, instead of healing their wounds, have only rubbed salt into them. If the authorities, by constructing walls and checkpoints around the localities where Hazaras live, have isolated them from other ethnic and sectarian groups, the fellow citizens have done so by displaying ethnic and sectarian hatred, thus falling for the 'divide and rule' policy of the ruling elite. Changezi, however, believes that terrorism and discrimination against Hazaras must not be seen in isolation. In 'Shootout at BMC' he tries to connect the miseries of the community with those people in Pakistan who have faced aftershocks of religious terrorism in some form or the other. He ensures the citizens that if they do not join hands to extinguish the fire of terrorism and discrimination burning the Hazara community, it will reach their houses as well and everybody will 'perish together as fools'.

Here it is pertinent to ask: "What has the community received from the country's security and justice systems as a solace for all their suffering?" Changezi believes that both the systems have miserably failed to offer anything tangible. Neither they did anything to stop the attacks, nor have they brought the culprits to justice. Security forces and intelligence agencies remained clueless during the peak of attacks on the community. Many of the attacks were carried out near the checkpoints created by Frontier Corps (FC) and police; however, the attackers were never caught. And after the attacks, investigations and operations promised with the community were never concluded, or they were never directed towards the terrorist groups, like Lashkar-e-Jhangavi though it had claimed responsibility for most of the attacks; rather they targeted Baloch separatists or 'ethno-nationalists'. Therefore, the community is still yearning for proper attention and true justice, which can at least heal some of their wounds.

Nevertheless, Changezi's writings have done justice to the ailing people by highlighting their plight and making their voices heard around the world. Similarly, the translators of his writings have done justice to his work. The translation seems impeccable; it maintains the flow in the writings and keeps their coherence and simple tone intact. Surely, this translation will convey the emotions, perceptions, and messages in the articles and stories to the English-reading audience in the manner perceived, expressed and intended by Changezi himself.

Sajjad Hussain (Aasim) is a PhD Scholar in International Relations and an avid researcher. His areas of interest include identity politics and political participation of ethnic minorities in Pakistan and Afghanistan.

'Unfinished Stories' reflects the consequences of symbolic violence

In Unfinished Stories, Hassan Raza Changezi provides captivating analysis of the trigger factors of terrorism and the deep roots of militancy in Pakistan, tracing back to historical, social and political processes. He further develops and illustrates this theme by providing historical and influencing factors behind the turbulent environment and the reality of the minorities, particularly the Hazaras. The overarching theme of the collection is politics and religion that are intertwined, leading to the State's inability to control the ensuing violence between the Shias and Sunnis as well as the persecution of the minorities.

With a particular focus on Quetta and the brutal killings of the Hazaras who reside in two segregated neighbourhoods with check-points and boundary walls, Hassan captures the experiences faced by the Hazaras. Although, the articles are not interpreted based on research, the author serves as a captivating storyteller based on his first-hand personal experiences from his childhood to the current reality of the Hazaras.

I first met Hassan when I was conducting fieldwork

for my PhD research on the Hazara community in Quetta in 2019. From our very first meeting, I was mesmerised by his eloquence and command of the Urdu language. Hassan is a respected author, blogger and political/cultural critic whose book Unfinished Stories is a compilation of articles. These were originally published in Dawn News blog in Urdu on social and political issues of Pakistan.

In the very first article, he draws on the fictional character of Sultan Rahi [Pakistan's Clint Eastwood] through reference to politicians with their 'fake promises' and ordinary citizens 'who are all ready to accept martyrdom'. In reality, these boastful claims have become indelibly familiar to us. Hassan packs a punch when he uses wit and satire for his social critique. In fact, in another article he relates people using social media to let off their frustration to the public toilet graffiti artists. Nevertheless, he does not ignore the significance of social media for the Hazara community; a powerful tool for activism and protest.

What makes the book a compelling read is the humour with undertones of the harsh realities such as terrorism and sectarian violence. Hassan uses irony in a humorous way to point out the deficiencies of the State and the establishment for the confinement of the Hazaras in the two cordoned off neighbourhoods and the terrorist's identities that remain a secret. The content of this conceptualisation sheds light on the notion of symbolic violence that has seen a rise in territorial stigmatisation and ethnic segregation. Hassan voices his concern on

233

silence on part of the ones in power, on the atrocities of the minorities even during the height of sectarian violence. But what is noteworthy about his contribution is that he echoes his own silence when his daughter repeatedly asks the reasoning behind the Hazara killings, considering there are many other Shia communities across Pakistan.

Most of the articles also reflect the consequences of symbolic violence that have led to a process of normalisation amongst different social groups, both the dominated and the dominant, or as I would term, the stigmatised and the stigmatisers. Hassan describes different strategies of the terrorist groups that resulted in mass injuries and fatalities, directly aimed at the Hazaras. He is not shy to criticise the spectrum of political leadership from industrial capitalism, feudalism to authoritarianism and politicization of Islam. Nonetheless, Hassan also recognises the resilience of the community by shedding light on the historic sit-ins of the Hazaras in sub-zero temperatures with the dead bodies of their loved ones that led to the imposition of Governor's rule in Balochistan.

I highly recommend reading 'Unfinished Stories.' The lucidity with which Hasan presents the collection as well as his flawless prose makes this a highly enlightening read. No doubt the insights contained in this book still relate to the current situation in Afghanistan and how it impacts Pakistan, particularly the Hazaras in Quetta.

Fatima Hashmi is a PhD candidate at Oxford Brookes University, Oxford. Her research centres on understanding the different forms of stigmatisation and populations' responses in a multi-side case study, focusing on the ethnic minority groups in Pakistan and Colombia. She has an MA in Development and Emergency Practice from the same institution with a particular focus on refugee studies and human rights.

Note: This review gives the views of Author, and not the position of Oxford Brookes University, or Centre for Development and Emergency Practice (CENDEP).

'The Unfinished Stories' depicts unfinished sorrows of the Pakistani Hazaras

Pakistan has been grappling with an existential threat of religious military extremism over the past forty years. The growing militant extremism which the Pakistan state utilised as its weapon of war against its regional foes, has now become the most prominent security threat to the Pakistani society itself. The militant extremist groups that were once located, managed, and trained for military activities outside the Pakistan borders in designated areas, now have spread and carved grounds within the settled areas of Pakistan. The militant extremist groups have transformed from militant outfits into complex militancy organisations, forging complex terrorist networks across the country.

Militarily, these extremist groups have demonstrated sophisticated behaviours and tactics in conducting acts of violence, at times, challenging the Pakistani military might. A large number of ideological/ religious organisations have become part of these networks, making significant contributions to the expansion of extremist discourses, narratives, and ideological grounds. The narratives that galvanise and promote a jihadi ideology have been the cornerstone of the growing religiously inspired militancy in and around Pakistan. Additionally, jihadi madrassas are crucial to the spread of religious extremism across Pakistan. This growing extremism in Pakistan is terrorising the society, leading fear to prevail hope. The Pakistani society is tattering on the brink of a collective nervous breakdown, which if remains unresolved, will have significant societal and security implications for the Pakistani state in the future.

In this growing wave of religious extremism and militancy, the Hazara community in Pakistan has been a prime target. The Pakistani Hazaras trace their ancestry to Afghanistan. Whilst there was already a consistent movement between Hazarajat [central highlands in Afghanistan] and India by the middle of the 19th century, before the first war between Britain and Afghanistan (1838-42), a mass migration from Hazarajat to India took place between 1880 1901. During this period (1880 1901), the Afghan King, Abdul Rahman Khan massacred around 63 per cent of the Hazaras in Afghanistan and forced a major chunk of the remaining populations into exile. The Hazaras who escaped Khan's violence sought refuge in the neighbouring countries, particularly in Iran and the Indian sub-continent. Following the creation of Pakistan as in independent state in 1947, the Hazaras were recognised as a tribe of Pakistan by the City Magistrate in Quetta on 15 June 1963:

This is to certify that, [the] Hazara tribe has been declared as a local tribe of Quetta Division by the Government of Pakistan.

The Pakistani Hazaras have been playing a significant part in the Pakistani society, including social, cultural, economic, and military. Despite contributing to the Pakistani society so much, the Pakistani Hazaras have been increasingly attacked by extremist groups since 1999, but targeted killings reached unprecedented levels in 2013, with some 700 Hazara murdered, many of those killed were in the province of Baluchistan. The death toll exceeded the previous high of 2012, described by Human Rights Watch as 'the bloodiest year for Shias in living memory.' As the violence against the Hazara community in Pakistan, especially in Baluchistan continues, everything is shattered for the community. Everyone appears to be struggling for their survival. Hope disappears, fear prevails. The violence has propelled the Hazaras in Pakistan in a crisis of trust and confidence in the state and in its apparatus that is bestowed by the country's Constitution to protect all its citizens.

The 'Unfinished Stories' is just all about the indiscriminate killings of the Hazaras in Pakistan, about their fear, mobility, and frustration that looms over their future. The 'Unfinished Stories' depicts the sufferings, sorrows, and horrors of the Hazaras in Pakistan, especially in Baluchistan province. The 'Unfinished Stories' provides a first-hand account of the ways in which the Hazaras are killed, and the ways in and through which the targeted